Great Americana

Travels in
Pensilvania and Canada

———————————————————————

John Bartram

Travels in
Pensilvania and Canada
by John Bartram

READEX MICROPRINT

Foreword

Observations...Made By Mr. John Bartram In his Travels from Pensilvania was printed in London in 1751. The trip described in the journal took Bartram from Philadelphia through Pennsylvania and New York to Fort Oswego on Lake Ontario. It provides one of the best descriptions of the American wilderness in the mid-eighteenth century.

John Bartram, though possessed of little formal education, had become intensely interested in botany and had educated himself in this field. Called by Linnaeus the greatest contemporary "natural botanist" in the world, Bartram was the friend of some of the most distinguished American colonists of his day and was the correspondent of scientists in Europe. He often traveled from his home near Philadelphia to observe the country and to collect plant specimens. In the summer of 1743 he accompanied Conrad Weiser to Onondaga, where Weiser was to arrange a peace between the colonists and the Iroquois Indians.

Bartram's journal abounds in descriptions of the country. Particularly interesting are his remarks about the Indians he met. He doubted that they had profited much from their contacts with the English. "I am sorry to say, their morals are little if at all mended by their frequent intercourse with us Christians, tho' I am persuaded it is not the fault of our religion but its professors." The bad effect of liquor on the Indians evidently caused Bartram some surprise. He noted that "an Englishman when very drunk will fall fast asleep for the most part, but an Indian, when merry, falls to dancing, running, and shouting." Bartram also worried about the way in which some English traders treated the Indians, because it tended to make them favor the French rather than the English. Bartram felt very strongly that all North America properly belonged to the crown of Great Britain. The mere garrisoning of isolated posts, "inhabited by no subjects of France but soldiers," gave that country no claim to the region, in Bartram's opinion.

A copy of Bartram's journal fell into the hands of Fleet Street printers without the author's knowledge. The publisher adopted a rather condescending air toward Bartram because of his lack of "literal education," but he acknowledged that "this plain yet sensible piece merits attention." The publisher also included a letter from Peter Kalm, a student of Linnaeus and friend of Bartram, who visited Niagara Falls in 1750 and wrote a description of it. A map of the town of Oswego accompanies the text. More information about Bartram and his travels is given by Ernest P. Earnest, *John and William Bartram* (Philadelphia, 1940), pp. 44-59.

Travels in
Pensilvania and Canada

OBSERVATIONS

ON THE

Inhabitants, Climate, Soil, Rivers, Productions, Animals, and other matters worthy of Notice.

MADE BY

Mr. *JOHN BARTRAM*,

In his Travels from

PENSILVANIA

TO

ONONDAGO, OSWEGO and the Lake ONTARIO,

In *CANADA*.

To which is annex'd, a curious Account of the

CATARACTS at *NIAGARA*.

By Mr. PETER KALM,

A *Swedish* GENTLEMAN who travelled there.

LONDON:
Printed for J. WHISTON and B. WHITE, in
Fleet-Street, 1751.

(Price *One Shilling* and *Six-pence*.)

BOOKS printed for JOHN WHISTON and BENJ. WHITE, in *Fleet-Street*.

(In one Volume Octavo, the second Edition, Price 5s. bound.)

I. THE History of the *five Indian Nations* of *Canada*, which are the Barrier between the *English* and *French* in that Part of the World: With particular Accounts of their Religion, Manners, Customs, Laws and Government; their several Battles and Treaties with the *European Nations*; their Wars with the other *Indians*, and a true Account of the present State of our Trade with them. In which are shewn the great Advantages of their Trade and Alliance to the *British Nation*, and the Intrigues and Attempts of the *French* to disengage them from us; a Subject nearly concerning all our *American Plantations*, and highly meriting the Consideration of the *British Nation*; with Accounts of several other Nations of *Indians* in *North America*.

By CADWALLADER COLDEN, Esq;
One of his Majesty's Council, and Surveyor General of New-York. Also,

(In Eight Volumes compleat. Price 1 l. 16s. *bound)*

II. The Modern Husbandman, containing the Practice of Farming, as it is now carried on by the most experienced Farmers in the several Counties of England, for every Month in the Year. Containing,

1. The Timber and Fruit Tree improved, or the best Practical Methods of improving different Lands with proper Timber.

2. Agriculture improv'd, or the Practice of Husbandry display'd, shewn by Facts perform'd on all Sorts of Land, according to the old plain, and the new Drill Way of Ploughing.

3. Chiltern and Vale Farming explain'd, according to the latest Improvements. By WILL. ELLIS, Farmer, at *Little Gaddesden* in *Hertfordshire*.

III. The *British Merchant*, containing the Sentiments of the most eminent and judicious Merchants of the City of *London*, concerning the Trade and Commerce of these Kingdoms; particularly that which relates to *France*, *Spain* and *Portugal*. Illustrated with Notes and Maxims useful to Trade in general. Compos'd by a Body of Merchants, and publish'd by Mr. CHARLES KING, in three Pocket Volumes, Price 9s.

PREFACE.

THE following Journal was kept by Mr. *John Bartram*, in his travels from his own house near *Philadelphia* to *Onondago*, and *Oswego* on the *Cadarakin* or *Ontario Lake*. It is a misfortune to the publick, that this ingenious person had not a literal education, it is no wonder therefore, that his stile is not so clear as we could wish, however, in every piece of his, there are evident marks of much good sense, penetration, and sincerity, join'd to a commendable curiosity. It was to gratify this disposition, and that of his correspondents request in *England*, that he undertook, after other expeditions, to accompany Mr. *Weiser* on the business of the government, and was honoured with the encouragement of some very judicious and generous noblemen *here*, since dead, and the friendship of the skilfullest botanists in *Europe*.

It may be proper to inform the reader, that the negotiations set on foot in the conferences here related, produced a congress at *Lancaster* in *Pensilvania*, begun the 22d of *June* following, which was attended with the wish'd for success, in an amicable adjustment of all differences between the parties, under the mediation of the governor of *Pensilvania*. This treaty was print-

B   ed

ed the fame year at *Philadelphia*, and is to be found in Mr. *Colden's hiftory of the 5 Indian Nations*. A book worthy of the readers perufal.

This journal was by feveral accidents prevented from arriving in *England* till *June* 1750, and is now made publick without the author's knowledge, at the inftance of feveral gentlemen, who were more in number than could conveniently perufe the manufcript. Had he intended it for publication he would have made it probably more entertaining and perhaps have retrenched fome parts that make the leaft figure in it.

The friend to whom he fent it, thought himfelf not at liberty to make any material alteration, though as it now appears, many who feek only amufement in what they read, will in thofe places be difappointed where only are treated of the feveral plants with which nature has bountifully covered the hills and valleys he travers'd, with the various qualities of the foil and climate.

But when it is confider'd, of how great importance an intimate acquaintance with the natural ftate of this vaft wildernefs, and its capacity of further improvement is to *Great Britain*, and how little the endeavours of our countrymen have yet advanced this work, while we are indebted to our moft dangerous rivals for the little we do know, who will, if poffible, repay themfelves by excluding us from all we do not actually cultivate, and leave us *that only* while they want power to take it from us : I cannot

but

but think this plain yet fensible piece merits attention. It is by pursuing the discovery of the interior state of this great continent, that we can scarcely fail attaining and end, the most worthy the aim of a great maritime power, honoured as well as strengthened by a fair progeny of the most flourishing colonies in the world, and of which a good *Englishman* with peculiar pleasure will find *P. Charlevoix* confessing (however unwilling to own any thing inconsistent with the glory of his country) *that* France *cannot behold them without Terror.*

Knowledge must precede a settlement, and when *Pensilvania* and *Virginia* shall have extended their habitations to the branches of the *Mississippi* that water these provinces, on the west side of the *Blue Mountains*, we may reasonably hope to insure a safe and easy communication with the most remote known parts of *North America*, and to secure the possession of a dominion unbounded by any present discoveries.

If this desirable prospect appear chimerical, because great and distant, it is at least true, that no obstacle can be pointed out, but what we may easily remove.

England already possesses an uninterrupted line of well-peopled provinces on the coast, successively begun within less than 150 years, she sees them every year augmented by an accession of subjects, excited by the desire of living under governments and laws formed on the most excellent model upon earth. In vain do we look for

an

an equal profperity among the plantations of other *European* nations becaufe every power has tranfplanted its conftitution with its people. This furprizing increafe of people is a foundation that will bear a mighty fuperftructure, we need no other proof than in the wonderful growth of one of the provinces, (*Penfilvania* I mean) which tho' the youngeft of all, yet being more particularly founded on the principles of moderation (*the firft of all political Virtues*) and every way fam'd for the wifdom and lenity of its government, is become the admiration of thofe who compare it with any thing related by hiftory, and the well-known refuge of —— *the opprefs'd and perfecuted*, who chearfully abandon their native foil to purchafe the incftimable bleffings of liberty and peace.

The inhabitants of all thefe colonies have eminently deferved the character of induftrious in agriculture and commerce. I could wifh they had as well deferved that of *adventurous in inland difcoveries*, in this they have been much outdone by *another Nation*, whofe poverty of country and unfettled temper have prompted them to fuch views of extending their poffeffions, as our agriculture and commerce now make neceffary for us to imitate. In this skilful Perfons may employ themfelves; but a more accurate obferver than our author will not readily be found.

The welfare of a colony concerns the country from whence it derives its origin, in nothing fo
much

much as in the quantity of land broke up for tillage, the natural confequence of extending the frontier fettlements. This is not only beneficial in proportion to the increafe of vent, among the new fettlers of comodities exported from the mother country ; but by preventing the additional hands from applying themfelves to fuch manufactures as may interfere with the commerce, *effectually hinders* a michief that might ftop the advantages reaped before. A jealoufy has long prevailed at home, of manufactures in *America*, and it has been ufual for our manufacturers on various occafions to exprefs this opinion in frequent applications to parliament, vainly hoping to force a confumption abroad from the weakeft of all refources, *prohibitary laws* : But the wifdom of the legiflature has provided the moft effectual, if not the only remedy, by encouraging the vent of the growths of *America*, and thereby engaging the inhabitants to employ themfelves in raifing them ; a conduct grounded on the invariable obfervation, that perfection in agriculture naturally precedes manufactures, wherever a country finds a market for its produce fufficient to provide itfelf with the latter.

Mr. *Kalm*'s narrative of his travels to the *Falls of Niagara*, is a proper fupplement to the journey to *Ofwego*, his voyage begins from that place, and caries us on further in the fearch of every thing worthy our notice in this country : This gentleman is well known to be

a

a man of worth and great skill in natural history, and his little piece besides the candour and veracity of the writer, derives a great value from its being the only account in our language of this ftupendous object. *P. Charlevoix* an Author of good credit, (*where the intereft of his nation and religion are unconcerned*) has given us a defcription perfectly agreeable to Mr. *Kalm*'s, tho' much lefs circumftantial: It was in 1722, *he* was on the fpot, and the heights had not then probably been taken by inftruments, for he feems to think it very difficult if poffible; He gueffes the great Fall to be 140 or 150 feet from a meafure taken by founding; and adds, that he has feen fmall birds flutter juft above the fall itfelf; we have likewife an account of this cataract *Phil. Trans.* Nº. 371. p. 69. *from Mr. Boruffan* tranfmitted by Mr. *Dudley*. Mr. *Boruffan* relates that the *Governor* of *Canada*'s fon the *Marquis de Cavagnal* had founded it, and fixed the perpendicular fall at 26 fathom, this was alfo in 1722.

I cannot help taking notice of the alarm Mr. *Kalm*'s arrival gave the *French* at *Niagara*. They are confcious their enjoyment of this Fort is a manifeft violation of the treaty of *Utrecht* tho they know the juftice of the *Englifh Nation* will not permit them to compell the *Seneka*'s againft their inclination to diflodge them.

Among other curious parts of Mr. *Bartram*'s journal are his thoughts (thrown together at the end) on the Origin of the *Aborigines* of *America*;

rica; these conjectures are short, and it is likely occurr'd to him casually, perhaps they are not all well grounded, or at most apply'd to any but the *Eskimaux*, however, the same sentiments on this subject have been supported by the learned *Grotius* in his treatise *de Origine Gentium Americanarm*, and in his reply to *J. de Laet*.

This question has long been agitated with great warmth, and every solution of it hitherto, has found opposers, because those who have engaged in the controversy have forgot, or wilfully mistook, that the point in dispute cannot reasonably be, whether it was actually peopled from one or more particular places? but whether it might probably be peopled consistent with the *Mosaick* history; other wise it would be hard to say, how all this enquiry has been so much confined to *America*, when the passage of the inhabitants to many other parts of the globe is attended with equal difficulties.

P. Charlevoix who has with great exactness abstracted the opinions and arguments of the writers on this subject, has observed, that besides the easy passage by sea from the coast of *Guinea* to that of *Brazil:* If it has not yet been demonstrated that the new world is contiguous to the old on the South, North-East and North-West, at least the contrary has not been shewn, so that the principal difficulties to be encountered, arise not from the want of a Passage, but from colour, manner, and language, which seem irreconcileable to any we are acquainted

quainted with on this side the Globe. But are
the *Negroes* in *Guinea* more similar in these re-
spects, to the rest of the world ? Let any one tell
me, why most of the *Africans* are black and
woolly-pated, and I will shew him why the *A-
mericans* are red and without hair on their chins,
and many parts of their bodies. After all are we
sufficiently acquainted with the utmost powers
of nature ? to be sure the offspring of the same
pair in 3 or 4000 years might without a super-
tural interposition become of various complexi-
ons, and suppose we were convinced of this,
may not the infinite power that created our first
parents, and miraculously wrought the con-
fusion of tongues, have thus distinguish'd
their posterity for purposes only known to his
infinite wisdom. I ought not to omit that *P.
Charlevoix* recommends a careful observation
of those *Amrican* languages, that have the
marks of being original, and a comparison of
them with those of *Europe*, *Asia*, and *Africa*,
and gives very judicious Reasons for depending
on a similitude in this, preferable to that of manners ; I shall only add, that Mr. *Lewis Evans*
a companion of our author's in this journey, and
a skilfull surgeon, has lately publish'd a map
of *New York*, *Pensilvania*, and *Jersey*, with part
of *Virginia*, *Maryland* and *New-England*,
chiefly founded on actual surveys. This map in-
cludes the route here described, which seems laid
down very exactly. And is sold by Mr. *Bowle's*
map and print-seller in *Cornhill*.

OBSERVA-

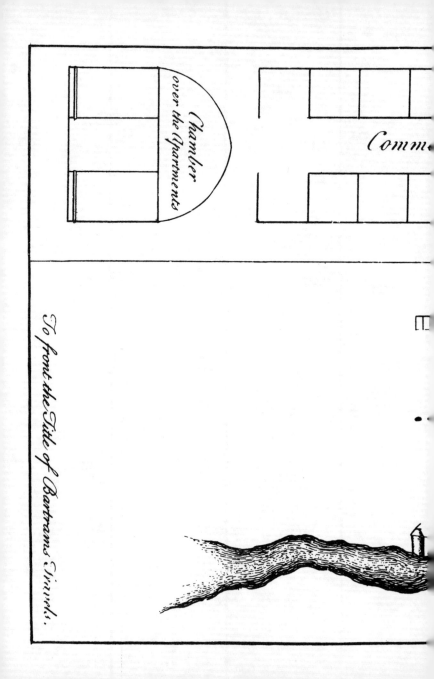

Chamber over the Apartments

Comm

To front the Title of Bartrams Travels.

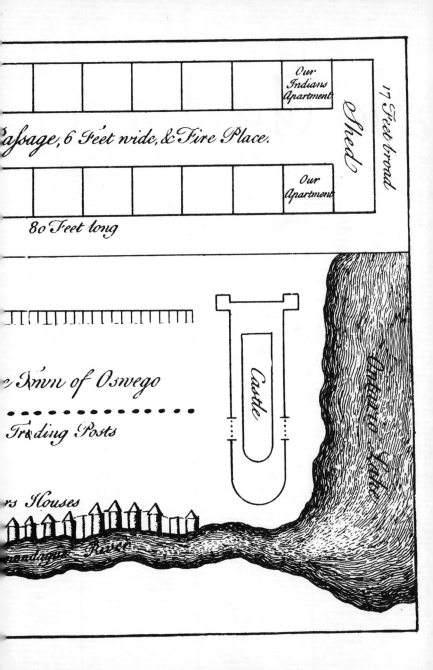

Our Indians Apartment

Our Apartment

Shed

17 Feet broad

Passage, 6 Feet wide, & Fire Place.

80 Feet long

e Town of Oswego

Trading Posts

s Houses

Castle

Ontario Lake

Onondague River

OBSERVATIONS

MADE BY

Mr. *JOHN BARTRAM,*

In his Journey from

Pensilvania to *Onondago,* &c.

HE 3d of *July* 1743, I set out from my house on *Skuylkil River,* with *Lewis Evans,* and travelled beyond *Perkiomy Creek* the first day. The weather was exceeding hot. The *4th,* we set out before day, and stopp'd at *Marcus Hulin's* by *Manatony*; then crossed *Skuylkil,* and rode along the west side over rich bottoms, after which we ascended the *Flying Hill,* (so called from the great number of wild Turkeys that used to fly from them to the plains) here we had a fine prospect of the *Blue Mountains,* and over the rich *Vale of Tulpehocken*; the descent into which is steep and stoney. Through this vale we travelled

west,

weſt, and by the way obſerved a large ſpring
16 feet deep, and above 20 yards wide, which
iſſued out of a limeſtone rock, the ground
about it pretty level, deſcending gradually
towards the ſpring which ran eaſtward. At
at night we lodged at *Conrad Weiſers*, who
is the general Interpreter, and who went with
us; his buſineſs was to ſettle an affair with the
Indians at *Onondago*.

The *5th*, We croſſed *Tulpehocken Creek*
which runs eaſt, and emptieth itſelf into
Skuylkil, and a little after a ſmall branch of
Swataro which runs Weſt into *Suſquehanah*.
Theſe two large creeks receive moſt of the
water of that great rich vale between the
Flying Hills and *Tulpehocken Hill*, from which
the vale and creek receive their names, and
is itſelf ſo called from the *Indian* word ſigni-
fying a tortoiſe, unto which the natives of
the country have conceived it bears ſome ſimi-
litude. And theſe two hills are the ſouthern
boundary of this fine limeſtone vale, many
hundred miles long, and from 10 to 20 miles
broad to the northern boundary formed by the
Great Blue Mountains.

Having called on a man who was to go
with us and carry part of our proviſions to
Shamokin, he could not get his horſe ſhod
that day, but we rode to *William Parſons's*
plantation, who received and entertained us
                                                very

very kindly; his house is about six miles from the *Blue Mountains*.

The 6*th*, we set forward and ascended the first *Blue ridge*, from the top of which we made an observation, *Conrad Weisers Hill* bearing south 20 degrees east, the northern prospect to two gaps, thro' which we were to pass to the *North Hill*, N. 30 deg. W about 10 miles distant. The top and south side of this ridge is midling land, half a quarter of a mile broad, and produced some wild grass, abundance of fern, oak and chesnut trees. Descending the North side we found it more poor, steep and stony, and came soon to the first branch of *Swataro* which runs between the ridges, and is 3 miles from the next branch, all very poor land; but on this second branch it is good low land, with large trees of 5 leaved white pine, poplar, and white oak, here we dined by a spruce swamp.

After dinner we passed the openings of two ridges, the last of which was by the bank of the principal branch of *Swataro*, the soil poor and stoney; then we ascended a great ridge about a mile steep, and terribly stoney most of the way: near the top is a fine tho' small spring of good water. At this place we were warned by a well known alarm to keep our distance from an enraged rattle snake that had put himself into a coiled posture of defence, within a dozen yards of our path, but

we

we punished his rage by striking him dead on
the spot: he had been highly irritated by
an *Indian* dog that barked eagerly at him, but
was cunning enough to keep out of his reach,
or nimble enough to avoid the snake when he
sprung at him. We took notice that while
provoked, he contracted the muscles of his
scales so as to appear very bright and shining,
but after the mortal stroke, his splendor became much diminished, this is likewise the
case of many of our snakes.

The north side of the Hill is not so stony as
the south, but yet very poor. Thence we
traveled 7 miles over several hollows, swamps
and small ridges, full of scrubby bushes,
and still poor and stoney to the last great
ridge, which is composed chiefly of large
gravel, as big as pidgeons or pullets eggs, and
even the rocks seemed but heaps of the same
materials; the descent on the north side is very
steepand rocky, large craggy rocks are disposed
on all sides, most part of the way down, which
brought us to a fine vale, where we lodged by
a creek called *Saurel*, and were grievously
stung all night with small gnats, so that I slept
very little.

The 7*th*, we set out west from *Saurel* creek
and traveled down the vale, which is pretty
good land: and leaving the creek, soon crossed
another runing along the north side of the vale,
by the bank of which we rode through a grove
of

of white Pine, very lofty aud fo clofe, that the Sun could hardly fhine through; at the end of this the two branches joined. Riding a little farther, we paffed through a gap of a moderate hill, north by the creek fide, where we found a fifhing place, moftly a deep hole near a rock; there we went weft on the north fide of the creek, and dined at what is called the *Double Eagle*. The land hereabouts is middling white oak and huckleberry land, and by the creek fide pretty good wild grafs, and the 3d branch enters about 30 rood below; having croffed this, we went up a vale of middling foil, covered with high oak Timber, nearly weft to the top of the hill, (moft of the way being a white clay under a fhallow furface), where we firft obferved the impreffion of fhells in fome of the loofe ftones, and from whence we had a fair profpect of the river *Sufquehanah.*

The defcent from hence foon brought us to *Mohony,* our lodging for this night. Here the foil is very good throughout the neck, formed by the river and the creek, which is about 3 poles wide. It rained this night through our old, tho' newly erected lodging, which was an *Indian Cabin* that we took the liberty to remove, knowing they ufually leave behind them a good ftock of fleas on the ground they inhabit; however, the wet deprived me of my

rest

reſt that I had taken ſo much pains to ſecure againſt the vermin.

July 8. We croſſed the creek and rode along a rich bottom near the river for two miles, producing moſt kinds of our foreſt trees, and a large ſpecies of *Scutelaria* two feet high : thence along the river ſide, near a mile N. 20 deg. E. to the foot of a fertile hill, where leaving the river, our way N. E. through ſeveral narrow valleys and over ſmall hills, generally middling land, yielding oak, hickery, cheſnut, and ſome pine, to the ſummit of a high hill, where we ſaw *Shamokin Hill*, diſtant four miles only ; going down we came to uneven ſtony ground producing pitch pine and oak, as far as the point of *Shamokin Hill*, whence we had a pleaſant proſpect of the fall of the river, quite croſs without any great Rocks. The ſtream runs very ſwift, but canoes or flat-bottomed boats may go up or down well enough : the bottom of this deſcent is waſhed by *Shamokin Creek* three rods wide , this we forded to a fruitful bottom half a mile wide, beyond which, two miles good oak land brought us to the town of *Shamokin.* It contains eight cabbins near the river's bank right oppoſite the mouth of the weſt branch that interlocks with the branches of *Allegheny.* It is by means of this neighbourhood that we may reaſonably hope, when theſe parts ſhall be better known, that a very

beneficial

beneficial Trade may be extended through
the *Hokio* into the *Mississippi* and its branches
among the numerous nations that inhabit their
banks. It were to be wished, that the *English* government in these parts had been more
diligent in searching and surveying the heads
of their own rivers and the sources of the
others that run westwards from the backs of
their respective provinces. Yet enough is already known to justify the surmises of *Mr.
de la Sale*, who in his Journal addressed to
the *Count de Frontenac* expresses his fears, lest
the *English*, from their settlements, should
possess themselves of the trade on the *Mississippi*. I quartered in a trader's cabbin, and about midnight the *Indians* came and called up
him and his squaw, who lay in a separate part
where the goods were deposited, whether together or no I did not ask. She sold the
Indians rum, with which being quickly intoxicated, men and woman began first to sing
and then dance round the fire; then the women would run out to other cabbins and soon
return, leaving the men singing and dancing
the war dance, which continued all the next
day. An *Englishman* when very drunk will
fall fast asleep for the most part, but an *Indian*, when merry, falls to dancing, running,
and shouting, which violent action probably
may disperse the fumes of the liquor, that
had he sat still or remained quiet, might have
made

made him drowfy, and which is even carries
off by continued agitation.

As foon as we alighted they fhewed us
where to lay our baggage, and then brought
us a bowl of boiled fquafhes cold ; this I then
thought poor entertainment, but before I came
back I had learnt not to defpife good *Indian*
food. This hofpitality is agreeable to the
honeft fimplicity of antient times, and is fo
punctually adhered to, that not only what is
already dreffed is immediately fet before a
traveller, but the moft preffing bufinefs is
poftponed to prepare the beft they can get for
him, keeping it as a maxim that he muft al-
ways be hungry, of this we found the good
effects in the flefh and bread they got ready
for us.

July 9. After breakfaft *Lewis Evans* and
myfelf went to the point of the mountain clofe
to the N. E. branch, a mile and half up the
river from our lodging, and good level rich
land all the way ; we walked thither, carrying
our blankets with us, and flept near three hours.
Here we regulated our journey, and having
taken a pleafant view of the range of mountains,
and the charming plane of *Shamokin*, 2 miles
long and above one broad, skirted on the Weft
and North by the river, and encompaffed Eaft,
and partly South, with lofty hills, befides a
fine vale bordering the North Weft branch,
we returned to the town and dined. In the
afternoon

afternoon. In the afternoon we borrowed a canoe, and paddled up the West branch. It is near two-thirds as broad as the North East or main river : I went afhore on the fouth fide to the point of a hill to look for curiofities, but found none ; the rock confifted of a dark coloured fhelly ftone. Then we diverted our felves with fwimming, the water was chin deep moft of the breadth, and fo clear one might have feen a pin at the bottom. At night I hung up my blanket like a hammock, that I might lie out of the reach of the fleas, troublefome and conftant guefts in an *Indian* hut ; but I found my contrivance too cool for a place open on all fides, tho covered with a kind of granary, efpecially the wind blowing cold from the N. W.

10. We departed in the morning with *Shickcalamy* and his fon, he being the chief man in the town, which confifted of *Delaware Indians*, he was of the fix nations, or rather a *Frenchman*, born at *Mont-real*, and adopted by the *Oneidoes*, after being taken prifoner; but his fon told me he was of the *Cayuga* nation, that of his mother, agreeable to the *Indian* rule *Partus fequitur ventrem*, which is as reafonable among them as among cattle, fince the whole burthen of bringing up falls on her ; therefore in cafe of feparation the children fall to her fhare.

D   We

We had many advantages from the company of thefe guides, were perfectly acquainted with that part of the country, and being of the fix Nations they were both a credit and protection; and, alfo as we went to accommodate the differences, and allay the Heart-burnings that had been raifed by a late fkirmifh on the back of *Virginia*, between fome of thefe nations and the *Englifh*, we could not but derive a confidence from the company of a chief.

We coafted the river near a mile to the ford, where we had a good bottom not above 3 feet deep; this brought us to an Ifland near 2 miles long and a quarter broad, pretty rich at the lower end, and near the river, but the higher end fandy, from the drift left there by the floods, it therefore produces little but *pitch pine*. After leaving the lower end where we faw feveral cabbins, we once more took water for the oppofite fhore, but the bottom is lefs even, though not above half as wide as the laft, which is about 400 yards.

Hence leaving the weft branch about half a mile on our left, and rich low ground between with gravel, oak and pitch-pine land on our right, we reached a pretty fpring of good water, fituated between the fwamp and dry ground. This, fince our paffage over the *Blue Mountains*, was the only one we met with till we came near *Onondago*, for on that
side

fide the currents and creeks are chiefly formed
by the water oufing and draining from the
bottoms of the mountains and hills, and are
gradually collected in this manner into rivu-
lets But on the fouth of this great ridge, it
gufhes out between the rocks in ftreams
big enough to turn a mill, in other places
rifing and bubbling out of the earth in quantity fufficient to fill a pipe an inch fquare, or
thereabouts.

Our journey now lay through very rich
bottoms to a creek 6 miles from *Shamokin*, a
great extent of fruitful low ground ftill con-
tinuing. Here we found a fine meadow of
grafs on our right, and rich dry ground on
the left. In our path lay a large Rattle-
fnake, but he civilly crept into the grafs, and
let us pafs by without danger. Our way from
hence lay through an old *Indian* field of excellent foil, where there had been a town, the
principal footfteps of which are peach-trees,
plumbs and excellent grapes. A great flood
came down this branch a few years paft, and
drove abundance of fand over this ground a
great depth among the trees. It rofe 20 feet
perpendicular, wafhing away many yards of
the bank, which was compofed of gravel and
fand, and doubtlefs had been raifed to that
heighth by former inundations, for the wood
ground 30 rod from the river is feveral feet

lower

lower than the bank ; a little above this deva-
ftation we dined.

And now leaving the river we held a new
courfe over a fine level, then down a rich
hollow to a *run*, where we faw a fummer
duck ; and fo down the *run*, a little beyond
this turns a path to *Wiomick*, a town on
the eaft branch, hence N. N. E. then N. after
W. to a rich bottom near the river, where
Shickcalamy formerly dwelt, at the upper end
of which refiftlefs torrents had carried abundance of fand into the woods. With this bottom we left the river for the prefent, and kept
a variable courfe through the gap of the
mountain N. and N. W. over middling cham-
pion land, producing fome pitch pine, and
large white and black oak, fome fwamps and
brooks, by one of which we lodged in a
fertile valley, that we reached before night.

11. About break of day it began to rain,
and the *Indians* made us a covering of bark
got after this manner : They cut the tree
round through the bark near the root, and
make the like incifion above 7 feet above
it ; thefe horizontal ones are joined by a
perpendicular cut, on each fide of which they
after loofen the bark from the wood, and
hewing a pole at the fmall end, gradually ta-
pering like a wedge about 2 feet, they force
it in till they have compleated the feparation all round, and the bark parts whole
from

from the tree, one of which, a foot diameter, yields a piece 7 feet long and above
3 wide : And having now prepared four forked
ſticks, they are ſet into the ground the longer
in front; on theſe they lay the croſs-poles,
and on them the bark. This makes a good
tight ſhelter in warm weather. The rain was
quickly over, but as it continued cloudy, we
did not care to leave our ſhed. Here our *Indians* ſhot a young deer, that afforded us a
good feaſt.

12. We ſet forward and travelled up the
Run, bearing N. W. along a narrow valley,
moderately rich, the hills hung with lofty
timber, the ſtones generally flat, then up a ſteep
hill, where I found foſſil ſteel in many ſtones,
the ſoil middling oak land; and here had a
view of a Bluf point N. by the river ſide;
then deſcending down a ſteep hill N. E. we
came to a rich bottom by the river; hence N.
after N. W. to a creek, and ſo through a grove
of white walnut and locuſt, and exceeding rich
land, half a mile broad, and now ſome higher
level land, affording oak, hickery, walnut, locuſt,
and pitch pine, our courſe generally N. N. W.
till riding over a hazel plane we met eight
Shawaneſe Indians on horſeback coming from
Allegheny, and going to *Wiomick* upon an im-
portant account, as they ſaid. We turned
back with them to the adjacent wood, and
ſate down together under a ſhady oak; the

ſquaw

fquaw which they brought to wait upon
them kindled a fire to light their pipes ; our
Interpreter and *Shickcalamy* fet down with
them to fmoke, the cuftomary civility when
two parties meet ; *Conrad Weifar* underftand-
ing they were fome of the chiefs of the *Shawanefe,* acquainted them with our bufinefs at
Onondago, a compliment they were fo well
pleafed with, that they gave us the *Yohay,* a
particular *Indian* expreffion of approbation, and
which is very difficult for a white man to imitate well ; after half an hour's grave difcourfe
feveral of them went to catch the horfes, and
one of the principal men made a handfome
fpeech, with a pleafant well compofed countenance, to our interpreter, to the following
effect : ' That they were fenfible with what
' an unwearied diligence he had hitherto been
' inftrumental in preferving peace and gocd
' harmony between the *Indians* and *White*
' *People,* and that as they could not but now
' commend the prudence and zeal with which
' he had effected this laudable purpofe, fo
' they earneftly entreated and fincerely hoped
' he would ftill perfevere in the fame endea-
' vours and with the fame fuccefs, and that his
' good offices may never be wanting on any
' future occafion.

The *Shawanefe,* or *Shaounons,* as they are
called by the *French,* are the fame people, the
Six nations : and at *New York* are called *Satanas* ;
they

they dwell upon the *Hokio* and to the southward of it, between whom and that of the *Cherokees* is a river sometimes called by that name. It was against this people the six nations first turned their Arms with success, after they had fled before warlike *Adarondacks*, and having thus learn'd to conquer, ventured to attack their hitherto victorious enemies, who could not have supported this war without the unexpected assistance they received from the *French*.

After taking our leaves, we continued our journey to a large creek 4 or 5 rod wide which washes on each shore a charming country of rare soil as far as the river. On the other side of this creek we rode through a deserted Town in the neck between them; a few miles more brought us to our dining place, and in the afternoon we turned our backs on this branch, and rode N. W. down a valley 20 rods wide, wooded with pitch pine on the right hand and white on the left, the *Run* between; then N. W. by W. by the side of a hill and bottom of white pine, down which we rode 2 hours, upon better land, the N. W. middling land, now up a hill N. W. to a point, a prospect of an opening bearing N. then down the hill to run, and over a rich neck lying between it and *Tiadaughton* bearing N. W. where we lodged within about 50 yards of a hunting cabin, where there were 2 Men, a Squaw and a child,

child, the men came to our fire and made us a
prefent of fome venifon, and invited Mr *Weifar*,
Shickalamy and his fon, to a feaft at their cabin.
It is incumbent on thofe who partake of a feaft
of this fort, to eat all that comes to their
fhare or burn it : now *Weifar* being a traveller
was intitled to a double fhare, but he being
not very well, was forced to take the benefit of a
liberty indulged him, of eating by proxy,
and called me, but both being unable to cope
with it, *Lewis* came in to our affiftance, not-
withftanding which we were hard fet to get
down the neck and throat, for thefe were
allotted us; and now we had experienced the
utmoft bounds of their indulgence, for *Lewis*
ignorant of the ceremony of throwing the
bone to the dog, tho' hungry Dogs are generally nimble, the *Indian* more nimble, laid
hold of it firft, and committed it to the fire,
religioufly covering it over with hot afhes.
This feems to be a kind of offering, perhaps
firft fruits to the Almighty power to crave
future fuccefs in the approaching hunting fea-
fon, and was celebrated with as much decency
and more filence, than many fuperftitious ce-
remonies : the bigotry of the popifh miffiona-
ries tempt them to compafs fea and land to
teach their weak Profelites what they call the
chriftian religion. To this I may add another
ceremony at bear hunting, as related by a
celebrated author, this diverfion being in the
winter,

winter, when this animal is very fat, the greafe
that fwims on the broth becomes a perfect oil,
which the *Indians* frequently drink untill
they burft —— As foon as the bear is
killed, the hunter places the fmall end of
his pipe in its mouth, and by blowing in
the bowls, fills the mouth and throat full of
fmoak, then he conjures the departed Spirit
not to refent the injury done his body, nor to
thwart his future fport in hunting, but as he
receives no anfwer to this, in order to know
if his prayers have prevailed, he cuts the liga-
ment under the bear's tongue, if thefe ligaments
contract and fhrivel up, being caft into the
fire, which is done with great folemnity and
abundance of invocations : then it is efteemed a
certain mark (as it rarely fails) that the *manes*
are appeafed. It was now time to return to
our fire where we laid us down to reft.

The 13*th*, in the morning, the *Indians* re-
paid our vifit, and entertained us with a fa-
miliar converfation for half an hour at the fire.
We then fet out up the creek, where I obferved
three noble white pine trees, with many large
green cones hanging on the top and fide branches
over the creek, which was three rods broad and
pretty deep, had thefe been ripe I know not
how we fhould have got at them, as they
were at the extremity of large branches, that
hung over the Water, on which part of the
branch they generally grow. Soon after we

E   came

came to a spacious level of midling land,
oak, and pine, next to a large rich bottom,
and at the upper end o an extensive grove of
white pine, after this a grassy plain of 20 acres,
then round the end of a hill, and along a valley, and run N. by W. high timber and good
land on the hill side N. then W. and lastly, at
half an hour after 8 N. here our *Indians* shot 2
young deer. The land and timber good, brown
soil, and the stones flat and gritty. From
hence going over a hill we saw a gap N. N.W.
and descending down a steep part of the hill
to the head of a stoney brook and hollow,
we made our way through it, it was full of
spruce and white pine ; at the bottom we
killed a rattle snake, then crossed the brook
and traversed a rich bottom N. N. E. the
upper end pine, spruce, oak, laurel, poplar
and chesnut, some limes, stoney and brown
soil, several times crossed the creek and over
rich bottoms and stoney hill sides with laurel,
pine, spruce and swamps, till towards night.
On the north side of a deep stoney yet rich
soil, I found roots of *Ginseng* ; at night we
lodged by a creek, and the two *Indians* that
feasted with us, who accompanied us to the
Cayuga branch.

The 14*th*, Having forded the creek we
kept generally a N. N. E. course, mostly along
rich bottoms interspersed with large spruce
and white pine, oak, beach and plane tree,
ginseng,

ginfeng, and many more. We frequently paſſed the creek (which was very ſtrong) for the mountains often clos'd on one ſide ; it was big enough to turn two mills. At 9 o'clock the *Indians* fiſhed for trout, but caught none, being provided with no other means of taking them but by poles ſharpened at the end to ſtrike them, and the water deep: at the foot of a hill we croſſed the creek once more, and rode along a fine bottom, full of great wild nettles. The timber was ſugar birch, ſugar maples, oak and poplar, our courſe N. W. continued till after 12 'clock, then followed the eaſt branch N. N. E. about a mile, all a rich bottom where we found a *Liching Pond*, where we dined, the backs parts of our country are full of theſe liching ponds, ſome are of black ſulphureous mud, ſome of pale clay, the deer and elks are fond of licking this clay, ſo that the pond becomes enlarged to a rood or half an acre, the ſoil, I ſuppoſe contains ſome ſaline particles agreeable to the deer, who come many miles to one of theſe places, there had been a great elk there that morning, but the *Indians* told us that many years ago ſome *Indians* quarrelled there, in the ſquable one loſt his life, and that this made the deer keep from thence for many years.

Now traveling up the run eaſt, we left it on the right hand, to go up a hill covered with ſpruce, oak ſpruce, lawrel, opulus, yew, with

ginſeng

ginfeng and ataliafhum in abundance, then
kept generally an eaft courfe, having feveral
hollows and fteep afcents and over many
boggy rotten places, fome laurel and very
high timber, then down the fide of a hill to
an old beaver dam, over which we paffed,
and then over a large level of very good
ground, tall timber and abundance of leather-
bark or *thymelea*, which is plentiful in all this
part of the country. Our lodging was in this
fpacious flat.

The 15*th*, We fet out a N. E. courfe, and
paffed by very thick and tall timber of beach,
chefnut, linden afh, great magnolia, fugar-
birch, fugar-maple, poplar, fpruce and fome
white pine, with ginfeng and maidenhair;
the foil black on the furface, and brown underneath, the ftones a brown grit, the way very
uneven over fallen trees, abundance of hollows,
and heaps of earth, turned up by the roots
of proftrate timber : hence it is that the furface is principally compofed of rotten trees,
roots, and mofs, perpetually fhaded, and for
the moft part wet, what falls is conftantly
rotting and rendring the earth loofe and fpungy,
this tempts abundance of yellow wafps to
breed in it, which were very troublefome
to us throughout our journey, on the branches
of *Sufquehanah* our courfe this day was generally eaft, and we got through this difmal
wildernefs about two hours before funfet, and
came

came to oak and hickery land, then down a
steep hill producing white pine to a creek called
Conuria a branch of *Towintohow*, where we
lodged in a bottom producing ginseng, sarea-
parilla mediola, maidenhair, darallia, panax,
mitela, christophoriana, with white, red and
blue berries, we had a fine warm night, and
one of the *Indians* that had so generously
feasted us, sung in a solemn harmonious manner, for seven or eight minutes, very different
from the common *Indian* tune, from whence
I conjectured it to be a hymn to the great
spirit as they express it. In the morning I
asked the Interpreter what the *Indian* meant
by it, but he did not hear him, and indeed I
believe none of the company heard him but
myself, who wake with a little noise, rarely
sleeping sound abroad.

The 16*th*, We began our journey up a little
hill, steep and somewhat stoney, and then
through oak, chesnut, huckleberries, and
honeysuckles, the land poor, sometimes white
pine, spruce and lawrel; thus far N. but at
half an our after seven N. E. through a great
white pine, spruce swamp full of roots, and
abundance of old trees lying on the ground,
or leaning against live ones, they stood so
thick that we concluded it almost impossible
to shoot a man at 100 yards distant, let him
stand never so fair. The straight bodies of
these trees stood so thick, a bullet must hit
one before it could fly 100 yards, in the most
open

open part. At half an hour after nine, we rode
down a small hill, and crossed a small run,
then climb'd a steep hill of oak land, and by
ten to a large creek called *Uskoho*, then round
the point of a hill, midling land, and up
the side thereof which was good, and
down the other side very steep to a *Run*,
with good corn land to the top of a hill in
sight of the east branch of *Susquehanah*, so far
we had pale clay land from the wilderness,
though blackish on the surface, for 2, 3 or 4
inches, then down half a mile on a moderate
descent, good oak and hickery land to a large
rich grassy and weedy bottom, 40 rood wide,
producing elm, birch, linden, lotus, white-
walnut, and very large white pine, where the
land is a little higher than common; at the
upper end of this bottom we dined at half an
hour after 12, we set out again at 3, course N.
along a steep hill side, full of excellent flat
whet-stones of all sizes, from half a foot, to 4
feet long, and from 2 inches to a foot wide,
and from half an inch to a foot thick; I brought
one home which I have used to whet my ax,
scythe, chizzels and knife, and is yet very little
the worse for wear, it is as fine as the *English*
rag, but of a blackish colour: this lasted two
miles close to the river which is here 100 yards
wide, and deep enough for flat-bottomed boats,
then we came to a very rich low land, most of
the way N. N. E. to the *Cayaga* branch, near
100 yards wide which we crossed, then rode
near

near a mile to the town-house, bearing N. this
town is called *Tohicon*, and lies in a rich neck
between the branch and main river: the *Indians*
welcomed us by beating their drum, as soon as
they saw us over the branch, and continued
beating after the *English* manner as we rode to
the house, and while we unsaddled our Horses,
laid in our luggage and entered our selves: the
House is about 30 foot long, and the finest
of any I saw among them. The *Indians* cut
long grass and laid it on the floor for us to sit
or lie on ; several of them came and sat down
and smoaked their pipes, one of which was
six foot long, the head of stone, the stem a
reed, after this they brought victuals in the
usual manner: here I observed for the first
time in this journey, that the worms which
had done much mischief in several parts of our
Province, by destroying the grass and even
corn for two summers, had done the same thing
here, and had eat off the blade of their maize
and long white grass, so that the stems of both
stood naked 4 foot high; I saw some of the
naked dark coloured grubs half an inch long,
tho' most of them were gone, yet I could
perceive they were the same that had visited
us two months before; they clear all the grass
in their way, in any meadow they get into,
and seem to be periodical as the locusts and
caterpillar, the latter of which I am afraid
will do us a great deal of mischief next summer. Here one of our hosts at the hunting
cabin

cabin left us to go up this branch to his own country, that of the *Cayagas*, this night it rained a little, and the morning was very foggy.

17th. Day, we crossed the neck to the east branch of *Sufquehanah*, up which we travelled along a rich bottom of high grass and woods of a fine creek, then over oak and pitch pine land to a swampy run and fine meadow ground, then east through white and pitch pine, oak, hickery and hazel bottom, and so N. E. to the river, where grew a white pine close to the water, with four green cones on, still we kept N. E. at 10 bore S. Here the river turned thus, occasioned by some high barren mountains on the other side, whose sides came close to it, and turned the stream in this crooked manner. We travelled through a fine vale of pine land. Here was a place where the *Indians* had been a *pawawing*. They cut a parcel of poles, which they stick in the ground in a circle, about the bigness of hop poles, the cicrle about five foot diameter, and then bring them together at the top, and tie them in form of an * oven, where the conjurer placeth himself; then his assistants cover the cage over close with blankets and to make it still more suffocating, hot stones are rolled in; after all this the priest must cry aloud, and agitate his

* Vide Capt. *Beverley's* hist. of *Virginia*, 8vo. a curious and useful work, and the Baron *Lahontan's* entertaining voyages in these parts.

his body after the moſt violent manner, till
nature has almoſt loſt all her faculties before
the ſtubborn ſpirit will become viſible to him,
which they ſay is generally in the ſhape of
ſome bird. There is uſually a ſtake drove into
the ground about four foot high and painted.
I ſuppoſe this they deſign for the *winged airy
Being* to perch upon, while he reveals to the
invocant what he has taken ſo much pains to
know. However, I find different nations
have different ways of obtaining the pretended
information. Some have a bowl of water,
into which they often look, when their
ſtrength is almoſt exhauſted, and their ſenſes
failing, to ſee whether the ſpirit is ready to
anſwer their demands. I have ſeen many of
theſe places in my travels. They differ from
their ſweating coops, in that they are often
far from water, and have a ſtake by the cage,
yet both have a heap of red hot ſtones put in.
at 11 we dreſſed our dinner, and found an
Indian by the river ſide, reſting himſelf; all
his proviſion was a dried eel ; this he made us
a preſent of, and we gave him a ſhare of our
dinner. Their way of roaſting eels is thus ;
they cut a ſtick about three foot long, and as
thick as one's thumb, they ſplit it about a
foot down, and when the eel is gutted, they
coil it between the two ſides of the ſtick,
and bind the top cloſe, which keeps the eel
flat, and then ſtick one end in the ground before a good fire.

F

At

At half an hour after one we set out, middling oak land but stony, yet no great rocks; at 2 N. E. then N. good land, a rich bottom and flat stones on rising ground; we crossed the *Owagan* branch about thirty yards wide. Then half a mile to the town so called, where we lodged, there is very good land in this neck between the branch and main river. A little before sun-set I walked out of town to regulate my journal; but the gnats were so troublesome I could not rest a minute. They bit my hands so cruelly I was forced to give over my purpose. These are so troublesome from sun-rising to sun-setting that we could not rest while we were eating our victuals without making several fires of wet leaves round us to keep them off.

18. This morning we sent an *Indian* with a string of Wampum to *Onondago*, to acquaint them with our coming, and the business we came about, that they might send messengers to the several nations to hasten their deputies to meet them as soon as possible, for this town serves the five nations as *Baden* does the thirteen cantons of *Switzerland*, with this difference, that *Onondago* is at the same time the capital of a canton.

We set out at half an hour after 9, and travelled till 6; this day our general course was N. and N. W. having fine level rich land most of the way, and tall timber oak, birch, beech

beech, afh, fpruce, linden, elm and herb hierophilon, hepatica and maidenhair in abundance. We lodged by *Front Creek* in a fpatious vale, and it looking like rain, we made us a cabbin of fpruce bark, but no rain came.

19. We rode over good level land : after we came to very fwampy bottoms, thickets and hills of fpruce, and white pine ; here were three ridges of fteep hills that run nearly E. and W. and with difficulty we rode over their fteep cliffs, which projected clofe to the creek. We were feveral times obliged to ford it backwards and forwards. Several runs come into the creek on both fides from between the mountains, Now we came to moft excellent level ground, than which nothing can be more fruitful, full of tall timber, fugar, maple, birch, linden, afh, and beech, and fhrubs, as opulus, green maple, hornbeam, hama m elis, folanum, goofterries and red currans triphilum in abundance. Here we dined by a pleafant creek and choice land. After dinner we foon began to mount up a pretty fteep hill, covered with oak, birch, afh, and higher up abundance of chefnut and fome hickery. This is middling land, the produce the fame for three miles as our land bears with us. It lies very high, and when cleared will have an extenfive profpect of fertile vales on all fides. We then rode down a long

rich

rich hill of moderate descent, where grew abundance of gooseberries, all the trees were crouded with wild pigeons, which, I suppose, breed in these lofty shady trees. I found many fossils on this hill.

Another fertile valley welcomed us at the bottom, over which travelling a mile we lodged at a *Run*, which our *Indians* told us emptied into the lake *Ontario*; if so, it must run into the *Cayuga* river, and so to *Oswego*.

20. We continued our journey in this pleasant vale until we ascended a hill, beyond which a slant brought us to two ponds that run into a branch of *Susquehanah*; crossing this we joined a part from the *Carugas* country; then over a rich level to another branch big enough to turn a mill where we crossed it. It was now three-quarters after 10, then good land to half an hour after 12 yet no hickery nor oak, but elm, sugar, maple, beech, birch, white walnuts, hop, hornbeam, and abundance of ginseng. After dinner we passed a branch of the great *Susquehanah*, down which lake canoes may go quite to where the river is navigable for boats. On the banks I found the *gale* like the *European*. This is the nearest branch of *Susquehanah* river to that of *Onondago*. Leaving this on our right, on our left we perceived a hill, where the *Indians* say *Indian* corn, tobacco and squashes were found on the following occasion :

cafion : An *Indian (whofe wife had eloped)*
came hither to hunt, and with his skins to
purchafe another here, he efpied a young
fquaw alone at the hill ; going to her, and
enquiring where fhe came from, he received
for anfwer, that fhe came from heaven to
provide fuftenance for the poor *Indians*, and
if he came to that place twelve months
after he fhould find food there. He came
accordingly and found corn, fquafhes and tobacco, which were propagated from thence
and fpread through the country, and this filly
ftory is religioufly held for truth among them.
Our way hence, lay over fine rich level land
as before, but when we left it, we enter'd a
miferable thicket of fpruce, opulus, and dwarf
yew, then over a branch of *Sufquehanah*, big
enough to turn a mill, came to ground as
good as that on the other fide the thicket ;
well cloathed with tall timber of fugar birch,
fugar maple, and elm. In the afternoon it
thunder'd hard pretty near us, but rained little :
We obferved the tops of the trees to be fo clofe
to one another for many miles together, that
there is no feeing which way the clouds drive,
nor which way the wind fets : and it feems
almoft as if the fun had never fhone on the
ground, fince the creation. About fun fet
it cleared up, and we encamped on the laft
branch of *Sufquehanah*, the night following it
thundred and rained very faft, and took us

at

at a difadvantage, for we had made no fhelter to keep off the rain, neither could we fee it till juft over our heads, and it began to fall.

One of our *Indians* cut 4 fticks 5 feet long, and ftuck both ends into the ground, at 2 foot diftance, one from another; over thefe he fpread his match coat and crept through them, and then fell to finging: in the mean time we were fetting poles flantwife in the ground, tying others crofs them, over which we fpread our blanket and crept clofe under it with a fire before us and fell faft afleep.

I waked a little after midnight, and found our fire almoft out, fo I got the hatchet and felled a few faplings which I laid on, and made a roufing fire, tho' it rained ftoutly, and laying down once more, I flept found all night.

21*ft*, In the morning when we had dry'd our blankets, we kept along the fide of a hill, gradually afcending, the foil good, timber tall, and abundance of ginfeng; here the mufquetoes were very troublefome, it being foggy, thence proceeding down a long gradual defcent on good rich foil with tall timber, fugar, maple, chefnut, cherry, linden and elm, we traverfed a large valley and rivulet, then rode up a little fteep hill where we ftopped at half an hour after eleven, this hill was a little fandy, with fome large pines growing upon it; here we walked and looked about us, having not had fuch an opportunity for two days, during

which

which time we had a fine prospect over the
vale of the great mountain we had just crossed,
and which differed so remarkably from all I
had ever been upon before, in its easy and fruitful ascent and descent, in its great width,
every where crowned with noble and lofty
woods, but above all, in its being intirely free
from naked rocks and steep precipices.

From these remarks, one might be naturally
led to imagine, that the Waters at the flood
gradually ebbed and retired on each side, towards the river *St. Lawrence* and *Susquehanah*,
the very next ridges on either side being nar-
rower, steeper, and some rocks washed bare,
and so all the adjacent ridges the farther they
are from this, appear to be more washed, more
composed of great banks of craggy rocks and
tremendous precipices, the soil more carried off,
mighty rocks tumbled down, and those left ap-
pearing as if piled up in a pyramid and hereby
preserved from a share in the awful ruin below
among their fellows; the soil being so perfectly washed from their root, as evidently no
longer to support them. After having enjoyed
this enchanting prospect and entertaining hypo-
thesis, we descended easily for several miles
over good land producing sugar-maples, many
of which the *Indians* had tapped to make
sugar of the sap, also oaks, hickery, white
walnuts, plums and some apple trees, full of
fruit; the *Indians* had set long bushes all round
the

the trees at a little diſtance, I ſuppoſe to keep
the ſmall children from ſtealing the fruit before
they were ripe: here we halted and turned our
horſes to graſs, while the inhabitants cleared a
cabin for our reception; they brought us
victuals, and we diſpatched a meſſenger immediately to *Onondago* to let them know
how near we were, it being within 4 miles.
All the *Indians*, men, women and children
came to gaze at us and our horſes, the little
boys and girls climbed on the roofs of their
cabins, about ten in number to enjoy a fuller
view, we ſet out about ten, and travelled over
good land all the way, moſtly an eaſy deſcent,
ſome lime-ſtone, then down the eaſt hill, over
ridges of lime-ſtone rock, but generally a moderate deſcent into the fine vale where this
capital (if I may ſo call it) is ſituated.

We alighted at the council houſe, where
the chiefs were already aſſembled to receive us, which they did with a grave chear-
ful complaiſance, according to their cuſtom;
they ſhew'd us where to lay our baggage, and
repoſe ourſelves during our ſtay with them;
which was in the two end apartments of this
large houſe. The *Indians* that came with us,
were placed over againſt us: this cabin is about
80 feet long, and 17 broad, the common
paſſage 6 feet wide; and the apartments on
each ſide 5 feet, raiſed a foot above the paſſage
by a long ſapling hewed ſquare, and fitted
with

with joists that go from it to the back of the house; on these joists they lay large pieces of bark, and on extraordinary occasions spread matts made of rushes, this favour we had; on these floors they set or lye down every one as he will, the apartments are divided from each other by boards or bark, 6 or 7 foot long, from the lower floor to the upper, on which they put their lumber, when they have eaten their homony, as they set in each apartment before the fire, they can put the bowel over head, having not above 5 foot to reach; they set on the floor sometimes at each end, but mostly at one: they have a shed to put their wood into in the winter, or in the summer, to set to converse or play, that has a door to the south; all the sides and roof of the cabin is made of bark, bound fast to poles set in the ground, and bent round on the top, or set aflatt, for the roof as we set our rafters; over each fire place they leave a hole to let out the smoak, which in rainy weather, they cover with a piece of bark, and this they can easily reach with a pole to push it on one side or quite over the hole, after this model are most of their cabins built, figure annexed.

The fine vale of *Onondago* runs north and south, a little inclining to the west, and is near a mile wide, where the town is situated and excellent soil, the river that divides this charming vale, is 2, 3 or 4 foot deep, very

full

full of trees fallen acrofs, or drove on heaps
by the torrents. The town in its prefent ftate
is about 2 or 3 miles long, yet the fcattered
cabins on both fides the water, are not above
40 in number, many of them hold 2 families,
but all ftand fingle, and rarely above 4 or 5
near one another; fo that the whole town is a
ftrange mixture of cabins, interfperfed with great
patches of high grafs, bufhes and fhrubs, fome
of peafe, corn and fquafhes, lime-ftone bottom
compofed of foffils and fea fhells.

It feems however, to have been more con-
fiderable when it became a conqueft to the
arms of *Lewis* 14th, at which time it muft
have been more compact, for hiftory relates
it to have been ftockadoed. The *Count de
Frontenac* governor of *Canada*, at the head
of the moft numerous army the *French* ever
drew together in *N. America*, had the fatisfaction in 1696 of triumphing over the afhes of
Onondago, whofe inhabitants terrified with
what they had heard of bombs, and generally
unwilling to hazard a fet battle, had already
abandoned their houfes after fetting them afire.
whatever glory the grand monarque might
reap from this exploit, it is certain he gained no other advantage, as a longer ftay
muft have inevitably ftarved the army, fo its
precipitate retreat helped our *Indians* to an
opportunity of taking their revenge by cutting

of

of every ftragling canoe, in their return by
water to *Monreal.*

At night, foon after we were laid down to
fleep, and our fire almoft burnt out, we were
entertained by a comical fellow, difguifed in
as odd a drefs as *Indian* folly could invent;
he had on a clumfy vizard of wood colour'd
black, with a nofe 4 or 5 inches long, a grining
mouth fet awry, furnifhed with long teeth,
round the eyes circles of bright brafs, fur-
rounded by a larger circle of white paint,
from his forehead hung long treffes of buffaloes
hair, and from the catch part of his head ropes
made of the plated husks of *Indian* corn; I
cannot recollect the whole of his drefs, but
that it was equally uncouth: he carried in one
hand a large ftaff, in the other a calabafh with
fmall ftones in it, for a rattle, and this he
rubbed up and down his ftaff; he would
fometimes hold up his head and make a hide-
ous noife like the braying of an afs; he came
in at the further end, and made this noife at
firft, whether it was becaufe he would not
furprife us too fuddenly I can't fay: I ask'd
Conrad Weifer, who as well as myfelf lay
next the alley, what noife that was? and *Shick-
kalamy* the *Indian* chief, our companion, who
I fuppofed, thought me fomewhat fcared,
called out, lye ftill *John,* I never heard him
fpeak fo much plain *Englifh* before. The jack-
pudding prefently came up to us, and an *Indian*

boy

boy came with him and kindled our fire, that
we might see his glittering eyes and antick
postures as he hobbled round the fire, sometimes
he would turn the Buffaloes hair on one side
that we might take the better view of his ill-
favoured phyz, when he had tired himself,
which was sometime after he had well tired us,
the boy that attended him struck 2 or 3 smart
blows on the floor, at which the hobgoblin
seemed surprised and on repeating them he
jumped fairly out of doors and disappeared.
I suppose this was to divert us and get some
tobacco for himself, for as he danced about
he would hold out his hand to any he came
by to receive this gratification which as often
as any one gave him he would return an awk-
ard compliment. By this I found it no new
diversion to any but my self. In my whim
I saw a vizard of this kind hang by the side
of one of their cabins to another town. After this farce we endeavoured to compose ourselves to sleep but towards morning was again
disturbed by a drunken *Squaw* coming into
the cabin frequently complimenting us and
singing.

22*d.* was a showery day, and we stirred
little out.

23*d.* we hired a guide to go with us to the
salt spring, 4 or 5 miles off, down the river,
on the west side of it's mouth; being most of
the way good land, and near the mouth very
rich:

rich: from whence it runs weftward near a quarter of a mile, a kind of a fandy beach adjoining to the bank of the river, containing 3 or 4 acres. Here the *Indians* dig holes, about 2 foot deep, which foon filling with brine, they dip their kettles, and boil the contents, until the falt remains at bottom; there was a family refiding at this time. The boys in the lake fifhing, the *Squaw* fetching water, gathering wood, and making a fire under the kettle, while the husband was basking himfelf on the fand, under the bufhes. We filled our gallon keg full of water and brought it to Town, where we boiled it to about a pound of falt. Our guides took their arrows, made of reed and down to fhoot fmall birds. About half way there is an excellent fpring of water, and by it a grove of *Curboroitæ* joining to a green fwamp, producing very high grafs. About a mile up the river from the lake, it runs by a fteep bank at the end of a high hill. The bank was fandy, and out of it run'd a brackifh water, which inclines me to think that there is a body of foffil falt here abouts, by which the plain is furnifhed with its intenfe falt brine, and that it is the vapour thereof that congeal| to the trafh and bufhes that lye on the bank, and glitters like flakes of Ice, or Snow, in a Sunfhiny day. This day 2 deputies arrived from the *Cayugas* Country.

24*th*,

24th. Lewis and I hired a guide to go with us to *Oswego* for 16*s.* our intention was more to get provisions for our journey home, than to gratify our curiosity. In the mean time, *Conrad* stayed at *Onondago,* to treat with the *Indian* chiefs about the skirmish in *Virginia*; with a view to incline them singly in favour of our application, before they assembled in council: and here I cannot help observing, it was scarcely ever known, that an *Indian Chief* or *Councellor,* once gained so far as to promise him interest, did break his promise, whatever presents have been offered him from another quarter.

We travelled on foot to the *Onondago* lake, whence we had fetched the salt water the day before, there we procured a bark canoe at half an hour after eleven, then paddled down the lake, and reached the lower end in two hours course, N. W. This lake the *French* call *Ganentaha*; hence we went down the river a mile N. big enough to carry a large boat, if the trees fallen into it where but carried away, this brought us to the river from the *Cayuga* country, near 100 yards wide, very still, and so deep we could see no bottom, the land on both sides very rich and low to within a mile of the *Oneido* river, where the river began to run swift, 'and the bottom became visible, tho' at a good depth. At three o'clock we came to the last mention'd river, down which the *Abbany* trader come to *Oswego*, half
a mile

a mile farther we came to a rippling, which carried us with prodigious swiftness down the stream, soon after we encountered a second, and a mile farther a third, very rough. In about an hour by the sun, after many other ripplings, we found our selves at the great fall, the whole breadth of the river which is above 100 yards wide and is eight or ten feet perpendicular: here we hawled our canoe ashore, took out all our baggage, and carried it on our back a mile to a little town, of about four or five cabins; they chiefly subsist by catching fish and assisting the *Alcany* people to hawl their *Bateans*, and carry their goods round the falls; which may be about ten or twelve poles, then they launch again into the river, and down the foaming stream that furiously on all sides dashes one half against the rocks, near a mile before they come to still water, and indeed, it runs pretty swift all the way to *Oswego*. These *Indians* were very kind to us, and gave us boiled corn and water melons, while they and our guide who was a relation sat over against us in the same cabin, chewing raw *Indian* corn stalks, spitting out the substance after they sucked out the juice. But we could not yet understand whether we were to go to the fort by land, or by water. In the morning they had catched some stout eels, and a great fish two feet long, it was round and thick, they strike them with long slender

shafts

shafts 18 or 20 feet long, pointed at the end
with iron see the shape. The 2 splints of wood
spreading each side, directs the point into the
fish, which at a great depth it would be otherwise difficult to hit. I saw upon one of their
canoes in the morning a large piece of bark
spread a-cross. On this lay gravel and sand,
and on these coals and ashes, which I supposed
had been a fire, and the gravel placed there
to save the bark. And I took it to be a de-
sign both to allure and see to strike the fish.

25th. Our guide, and several other *Indians*,
lead us to the canoes belonging to the town,
into one of which we got full of hopes of going by water, but were much chagrin'd to find
ourselves only paddled cross the water, where
we unwillingly took out our cloaths, victuals
and blankets, and carried them on our backs
following our guides, who were now increased
to three. We had 12 miles down the river by
land, most of the way middling land, some
white pine and spruce groves to pass through,
but most of the way in sight of the river,
which is very rapid most of the way to the
lake. On the point formed by the entrance
of the river, stands the fort or trading castle,
it is a strong stone house, incompassed with a
stone wall near 20 feet high, and 120 paces
round, built of large squared stones; very curious for their softness, I cut my name in it
with my knife. The town consists of about

70 log-

70 loghouses, of which one half are in a row near the river, the other half opposite to them, on the other side of a fair were two streets divided by a row of posts in the midst. Where each *Indian* has his house to lay his goods, and where any of the traders may traffick with him. This is surely an excellent regulation for preventing the traders from imposing on the *Indians*, a practise they have been formerly too much guilty of, and which has frequently involved the *English* colonies in difficulties, and constantly tended to depreciate us in the esteem of the natives ; Who can scarcely be blamed for judging of a nation, by the behaviour of those with whom they have the most intercourse. a judgment I am sorry to confess that has (till lately) tended much to the making them in favour rather of the French, than English. I speak of private persons, not of the respective government. The chief officer in command at the castle, keeps a good look out to see when the *Indians* come down the lake with their poultry and furrs, and sends a canoe to meet them, which conducts them to the castle, to prevent any person inticing them to put ashore privately, treating them with spirituous liquors, and then taking that opportunity of cheating them. This officer seems very carefull, that all quarreling, and even the least misunderstanding, when any happens, be quickly made up in an amicable manner, since a speedy

accom-

accomodation can only prevent our country
men from incuring the imputation of injustice,
and the delay of it would produce the disagree-
able consequences of an *Indians* endeavouring
to right himself by force.

Oswego, is an infant settlement made by the
province of *New-York*, with the noble view
of gaining to the crown of *Great Britain* the
command of the 5 lakes, and the dependence
of the *Indians* in their neighbourhood, and to
its subjects the benefit of the trade upon them,
and of the rivers that empty themselves into
them. At present the whole navigation is carried
on by the *Indians* themselves in bark canoes,
and there are perhaps many reasons for desiring
it should continue so for some years at least;
but a good englishman cannot be without
hopes of seeing these great lakes become one
day accustomed to *English* navigation. It is
true, the famous fall of *Niagara*, is an insurmountable bar to all passage by water, from
the lake *Ontario*, into the lake *Erie*, in such
vessels as are proper for the secure navigation
of either; but besides, that bark canoes are
carried on mens shoulders with ease, from one
to the other, as far as the passage is impracti-
cable: It will be much more easy to carry the
goods in waggons, from the upper lake,
into the *Huron* or *Quatoghie* lake, the strait
is rendered unnavigable by the *Saute St. Marie*,
but a vessel of considerable burthen may sail
from

from the hither end of the *Erie* lake, to the bottom of the lake *Michigan*, and for ought we know, through all parts of the 3 middle lakes. These lakes receive the waters of many rivers, that in some places approach so near the branches of the vast river *Mississippi*, that a short land carriage supplies the communication. And here to use the words of a most judicious writer, " He that reflects on the natural state " of that continent must open to himself a " a field for traffick in the southern parts of *N.* " *America*, and by the means of this river " and the lakes, the imagination takes into " view such a scene of inland navigation; as " cannot be paralleled in any other part of " the world. "

The honour of first discovering these extensive fresh water seas, is certainly due to the *French*, who are at this time in possession of settlements at *Fort Ponchartrian*, on the strait between *Lake Erie* and the *Lake Huron* and at *Mississimahinac* between the latter and the upper lake, but as these can give them no title against the original inhabitants or the *five nations*, Conquerors of all the adjacent nations, so it is difficult to conceive by what arguments these small posts, inhabited by no subjects of *France* but soldiers, can be extended to mark any possession beyond the reach of their gun's, or land actually cultivated, except by such as must intitle the crown of *Great*

Britain

Britain to all *North America,* both as *prior discoverers* and prior planters, without a subsequent desertion.

The traders from *New York* come hither, up the *Mohawks* river, which discharges itself into *Hudsons* river ; but generally go by land from *Albany,* to *Schenectady* about 20 miles from the *Mohawks* river, the carriage is but 3 miles into the river that falls into the *Oneido* lake, which discharges itself by the *Oneido* river, into the *Onondago* river, and brings their goods to *Oswego* in the manner I have before related.

We came to the town about 12 o'clock, the commissary invited us to the castle where we dined, together with the Doctor and Clerk. After dinner we had the satisfaction of swimming in the lake *Ontario,* which is some times called by our *Indians Cadarakin,* this is also the name of a french fort upon it, almost opposite to *Oswego,* N. it has 4 bastions built of stone, and is near half a mile in circumference; it stands where the waters of this lake are already formed into the river St. Lawrence, which makes a good road for great barks under the point of *Cadarakin Bay.* The famous and unfortunate Mr. *De la Sale* had two barks which remains sunk there to this day.

These lakes are said to have a kind of flux and reflux peculiar, since it is affirmed to be sensibly ebb and flood several times in a quarter of an hour, tho' it be perfectly smooth and
scarce

fcarce any wind. But it is evident from the face of the earth, that the water of the lake *Ontario* is confiderably diminifhed and has loft ground a great number of years, for the fhores above a mile within land, are abundantly more low, as well as of a loofer texture then the foil beyond, whether this effect is in common to all the waters on the earth, according to a conjecture of the great Sir *Ifaac Newton:* Or whether it be not at (leaft in part) owing to the removal of fome great obftruction, which by caufing a fall in the river St. *Lawrence,* might formerly pen the waters up to a greater height than now; or only to the gradual wearing away by the perpetual paffage of the water over thofe falls that ftill fubfift: or to a cafual ruin of fome part of one of them, I fhall leave to the determination of a more able naturalift than myfelf.

The water was very clear and as cold as our river in May, it is well tafted and fuppofed to be 120 miles broad, and near 200 long, ftreaching N. N. W. but this muft be an error, the common maps giving it a bearing to the Northward of the lake, but Mr. *Bellin* fhews us it lies E. and W. from the obfervations of *P.Charlevoix,* on the exactnefs of which he thinks he cannot too much relie, and *Bellin* in his map of thefe lakes has given it this bearing

bearing. We lodged in the caftle in the captains chamber.

26th. Early in the morning I walked out looking for plants, as I had done the evening before. I obferved a kitchen garden and a grave yard to the S. W. of the caftle; which puts me in mind that the neighbourhood of this lake is efteemed unhealthful, we were entertained by one of the traders, with whom we breakfafted; and bought of him fome dryed beef. And a gallon of Rum we got at the caftle. The traders had difpofed of moft of their bifcuit and had packed up their provifion, in order to return directly to *Albany* : however, one of them went about to the reft and collected us a good parcel of bifcuit; a kindnefs we were very fenfible of. After breakfaft I regulated my journal, having a convenient private room to do it in. We dined at the caftle, and at 3 o'clock fet out for *Onondago.* Two *Indians* helped to carry fome of our baggage; the day was warm, the *Indians* walked faft, our load was heavy and we were fufficiently weary before we reached the town near the falls, which was about fun fet. Indeed we had the favour of fhady woods all the way, we lodged where we did before. The *Indian Squaws* got very drunk and made a fad noife till morning. My fear leaft our guide was drunk alfo, added a good deal to an indifpofition I was feiz'd with in the evening, but

but in the morning I found him and his companion, to my great joy, faft afleep by the
outfide of the cabin.

27th, We fet out early and found our
canoe fafe where we left it, and it was with
much fatisfaction that I entered it. At half
an hour after ten, we got to the firft fall, above
the great oné, the *Indians* brought the canoe to
fhore and made fign for us to difembark and
walk along afhore, while they ftept into the
river, and hawled the canoe up the fall about
a quarter of a mile, by good land. We reim-
barked again, and at twelve came to the *Oneido* branch, up which the *Albany* traders return, after 2 or 3 months trade at *Ofwego-
Caftle* At 3 o'clock we entered the *Onondago*
lake, the upper end of which we gained by five,
the land about the lake is pretty good and fome
large marfhes and rich low ground moftly on
each fide, but here and there the hills come
clofe to the water: I think it muft be eight
miles long and above one broad, very brackifh
at the falt plain; very deep in fome places
near the middle, but fhallow for 100 yards
from the fhore. The *Indians* paddled the canoe a little way higher up the ftream and might
have brought us to the town, if the fallen
trees had been removed; but whatever nature
has done for them (and fhe is no where more
bountiful) they are too lazy by any trou-
ble of their own to improve; but when com-
pelled by the moft urgent neceffity. We

We reached the town about fun-fet, equally pleafed with our having improved the opportunity fo well by feeing *Ontario* lake, and that we were returned fafe to the interpreter and *Indian Chiefs*; thofe two laft days had been pretty warm: our *Indian* guide was a fullen, illnatured, and I believe, a fuperftitious fellow. Every now and then as we paddled up the river, he would with a compofed countenance utter fomewhat pretty loud for about the fpace of two minutes at a time, whether it was a magical incantation, or a prayer, I can't tell; I am fatisfied it was no fong, nor any fpeech directed to us, or the *Indian* with him, for he feemed intirely unmoved all the time.

28*th*, This was a rainy thundering warm day, and two deputies arrived from the *Oneidoes*. News came that the worms had deftroyed abundance of corn and grafs in *Canada*. This night we were troubled with fleas, and what was worfe, our men exceeding drunk and noify; our grievances in the day were more tolerable, being only women infefting us with their company and bawling, in great good humour, indeed I perceived to no quarrel while among them.

29*th*, Several more deputies arrived from the *Tufcaroroes*, we went to vifit a poor emaciated *Indian*, who they faid was bewitched, he lived about a mile from the *Council-Houfe*.

This

This day was warm, and several showers passed by to the southward.

30*th*, Three of the *Mohawks* arrived, this nation dwells farthest within the province of *New-York*, and to the southward of the river known by their name ; abundance of whites live among them, and as they are the best acquainted with the manners of the *English*, so they have at all times shewn the most steady affection to our people. I am sorry to say, their morals are little if at all mended by their frequent intercourse with us Christians, tho' I am persuaded it is not the fault of our religion but its professors, perhaps this may be esteemed a principal cause why they are become less numerous than any of their confederates.

This morning after breakfast, I went to the east hill, and found a fine spring on the west side, surrounded with *Arbor Vitæ*, some a foot diameter, this water is of such a petrifying nature, that as it runs among the fallen leaves it incrusts them and petrifies in great stones as big as one can well lift; there was a great piece of ground covered with them, which had turned the water-course several times, I have seen three of these springs in my travels; one on the other side of *Potomack* and one up *Delawars* at *Menesinks*; this hill is good limestone land, producing sugar maple, elms, beech, and some white pine, which

I   last

laft had then 3 or 4 cones, on 2 or 3 trees, but they were quite green.

This afternoon the chiefs met in council, and three of them fpoke for near a quarter of an hour each, two of thefe while fpeaking, walked backward and forward in the common paf-fage, near 2 thirds of its length, with a flow even pace, and much compofure and gravity in their countenance; the other delivered what he had to fay fitting in the middle, in a grace-ful tone exhorting them to a clofe indiffoluble amity and unanimity, for it was by this per-fect union their forefathers had conquered their enemies, were refpected by their allies, and honoured by all the world; that they were now met according to their antient cuftom, tho' feveral imminent dangers ftood in their way, mountains, rivers, fnakes and evil fpirits, but that by the affiftance of the *great Spirit* they now faw each others faces according to appointment.

This the interpreter told me was the opening of the diet, and was in the opinion of thefe people abundantly fufficient for one day, fince there is nothing they contemn fo much as precipitation in publick councils; indeed they efteem it at all times a mark of much levity in any one to return an immediate anfwer to a ferious queftion however obvious, and they confequently fpin out a Treaty, where many points are to be moved, to a great length of
time,

time, as is evident from what our conference
with them, produced afterward at *Lancaster*
begun the 22d of *June* 1744.

This council was followed by a feaft, after
4 o'clock we all dined together upon 4 great
kettles of *Indian* corn foop, which we foon
emptied, and then every chief retired to his
home.

3 1*ft*, In the morning, as foon as light, I
walked out to look at our horfes as ufual,
and clofe by a cabin fpied a knife almoft
covered with grafs; I fuppofed it loft, but
the *Indians* being not yet ftiring let it lie:
a little after fun-rife I walked there again,
and the *Squaw* being at the door, fhewed
her where it lay, at which fhe feemed exceeding pleafed, and picked it up immediately.
As I came back to our cabin, I fpy'd 2 *Indian*
girls at play with beans, which they threw
from one to the other on a match coat fpread
between them; as they were behind our cabin, I turned to fee how they play'd, but
they feemed much out of countenance, and
run off in an inftant: I obferved that the *Indian* women are generally very modeft.

About noon the council fat a 2*d* time, and
our interpreter had his audience, being charge
by the governor with the conduct of the treaty.
Conrad Weifer had engaged the *Indian* fpeaker
to open the affair to the chiefs affembled in
council; he made a fpeech near half an hour,

and

and delived 3 broad belts and 5 ftrings of *Wampum* to the council, on the proper occaſions. There was a pole laid a-croſs from one chamber to another over the paſſage, on this their belts and ftrings were hung, that all the council might ſee them, and here have the matters in remembrance, in confirmation of which they were delivered : The conference held till 3, after which we dined , this repaſt confiſted of 3 great kettles of *Indian* corn ſoop, or thin homony, with dry'd eels and other fiſh boiled in it, and one kettle full of young ſquaſhes and their flowers boiled in water, and a little meal mixed ; this diſh was but weak food, laſt of all was ſerved a great bowl, full of *Indian* dumplings, made of new ſoft corn, cut or ſcraped off the ear, then with the addition of ſome boiled beans, lapped well up in *Indian* corn leaves, this is good hearty proviſion. After dinner, we had a favourable anſwer, coroborated by ſeveral belts of *Wampum*, with a ſhort ſpeech to each, theſe we carried away as our tokens of peace and friendſhip, the harangue concluded with a charge to ſit ſtill as yet, for tho' they had diſpatched our buſineſs firſt, it was not because they were weary of us, but to make us eaſy. This conrplement preceded other buſineſs, which laſted till near ſun ſet, when we regaled on a great bowl of boiled cakes, 6 or 7 inches diameter, and about 2
thick,

thick, with another of boiled squash; soon after, the chiefs in a friendly manner took their leave of us, and departed every one to his lodging: this night we treated two of the chiefs that lived in the council hall, which as I mentioned, was our quarters; they drank chearfully, wishing a long continuance of uninterrupted amity between the *Indians* and *English.*

August 1. Six of the *Anticoque Indians* had an audience, but when they came to it, could not make themselves understood, tho' provided with an interpreter brought near 700 miles, (they said more) but he could not understand the *Mohawk* Language, but only the *Delawar* and middling *English,* * so they contrived he should direct his speech to *Conrad Weisar* in *English*, and interpret this to the council. They gave broad belts of *Wampum*, 3 arm belts and 5 strings; one was to wipe clean all the blood they had spilt of the *five nations*, another to raise a tumulus over their graves, and to

pick

---

* *P. Charlevoix*, perhaps from his own knowledge and the information he has received from his brother missionaries, tells us, that the languages of the northern part of *North America*, are properly 3, the *Sioux* or *Nadouissiour*, called by the *English Norway*, the *Algonquin* or *Adirondack*, and the *Huron* or *Quatoghie* of which last he makes the *Iroquois* called by our author the *Mohawk*, a dialect; but adds, he knew not what language is talked by the *Cherokees*, whether the language of the *Antecoques* be a dialect of the last which is very possible, or of the *Adirondack* which I take the *Delawar* to be, I can't determine.

pick out the sticks, roots or stones, and make
it smooth on the top, a third, to cleanse the
stomach of the living from gall or any thing
else that made them sick; a fourth was a
cordial to chear up their spirits; a fifth, to
cloath their bodies and keep them warm,
a sixth, to join them in mutual friendship, a
seventh, to request them to let them settle on
a branch of *Susqehanah*, another to intreat the
5 nations that they would take a little care
to protect their women from insults while out
a hunting, and the rest for such like purposes.
This business lasted 4 hours, then we dined
on *Indian* corn and squash soop, and boiled
bread. In the afternoon, I went on the
western mountain as I had the day before on
the eastern; it was very rich and full of tall
timber quite to the top, the trees were linden,
elm, sugar-maple, white walnut, oak, hickery
and chesnut, besides ginseng, and most sort of
herbs that grow on our rich lime-stone land.

These 2 days the wind was south and warm
and several showers to the S. E. The council
met at 9 o'clock, and the kettles of soop and
a basket of dumplings were brought in for
our dinner; after dinner the *Anticoques* delivered a belt and a string of *Wampum*, with
a complaint that the *Marylanders* had deposed
their king, and desired leave to chuse one for
themselves: to this, as well as all the articles
opened yesterday, the chiefs returned plausible
but

but fubtil anfwers; then they gave us 2 ftrings
withal, telling us, that now they had thrown
water on our fire, and we were at liberty to
return home when we pleafed, they all took
their leave, and bid us adieu by fhaking hands
very kindly, and feemingly with much affection.   This night the young men getting into
liquor, kept fhouting and finging till morning.

   3*d*, We prepared for fetting forward, and
many of the chiefs came once more to take
their farewell; fome of them brought us provifion for our journey, we fhook hands again
and fet out at 9.

   It was greatly to my mortification, that I
was forced to return for the moft part the
fame way I came. We had intended to go
through the *Mohawks* country to *Albany*, but
our 2 *Indians* could not be perfuaded to go that
way, tho' we offered to bear their charges,
and the chiefs were not willing we fhould leave
them to pafs through the wildernefs alone,
as they came to gratify us and further our
bufinefs. This day was fair, and the wind S.
In the afternoon, we afcended that lovely
mountain S. W. which divides the waters that
render tribute to the great ftreams of *St. Lau-
rence* and *Sufquehanah*. We did not directly
crofs the mountain, but rode a fmall way on
its fummit under the grateful fhade of thofe
lofty trees that every way adorn it; and
                                          after-

afterwards we traveled several miles on its S. W. side, where we enjoyed a fine prospect of a spacious rich vale on our left hand. On this hill we saw a lime stone a little bigger than my head, which is rare in these parts.

We entered the vale at 5, then crossed a *run* and rode along a rich level for several miles, and under the delightful protection of very tall trees that brought us to a creek, a branch of *Susquehanah*, where we lodged surrounded by ginseng.

4th, This was a fine day, and our traveling cool, because shady, and the goosberries being now ripened, we were every now and then tempted to break off a bough and divert ourselves with picking them, tho' on horseback.

5th, This morning was clear and cool, and now our journey was truly charming, it is scarce possible to think the advantage we had in returning from the single circumstance of being free from those small gnats that tormented us in our going so grievously. But our return being mostly in the same path, it will be needless to describe the land or its productions again.

6th, We set out an hour before sunrise, the morning clear, at half an hour after ten we reached *Owagan*, and turned our horses to grass, while we stopped at a cabin. The *Squaw* brought in a bowl of huckle-berries,

to

to stay our stomachs, and soon after a large
kettle full of small homony boil'd in strong
venison broth; this was noble entertainment,
and too good to leave any of. I heartily
pityed the poor *Squaw*, for I believe she had
dressed it for herself and several children: she
also obliged us to accept of a fine piece of
venison to carry away. Here we killed a rattle snake, the second we had seen to day: at
one we continued our journey through groves of
pine of a stupendous stature; the land midling for 2 miles S. W. to the river, then a
variable course over land of equal goodness,
oak and hickery, some bottoms rich; and by
three we cross'd a fine creek where we spyed
a grey squirrel which our *Indian* would have
shot, had it not been on the top of a white
oak: here we found very stony ground, great
stones having been drove by one common
force, into a form like that of fish scales,
yet this was a mile from the river, and many
yards perpendicular above the bed of it, this
may be the effects of the universal deluge, or
some mighty torrent of water since that, must
have flowed over these stones and washed them
thus bare. We travelled till about two hours
by the sun, and then pitched by the river,
which run full W. there was high barren
mountains on the upper side, here the river
was deep and smooth enough for flat bottom'd
vessels, which made us heartily wish that we

K   were

were in a canoe, and our horses at *Shamokin*, for we dreaded the dismal wilderness between. We observed here an old log, which the bears had cunningly turned to pick up the snails, beetles, and grubbs, that had crept under it for shelter.

7th, We rod over middling land, producing oak, pine, and great magnolia, to the *Tohicon* town on the *Cayugo* branch; this place we arrived at by noon but stayed there all night, frighted by several showers that passed over the mountains in sight: indeed it rained a little here, I walked to the branch after dinner, and found abundance of fossils on the banks, but the distance of the way, and heavy load of our baggage, were an insurmountable bar to my bringing any home. This day the *Anticoque* interpreter that travelled with us from *Onondago*, who left the path a little to hunt, misd our tract and hit upon an *Indian* town, 3 miles up the branch, and there picking up a *Squaw* brought her with him. The chief man of the town came to visit us in a very friendly manner, and our interpreter telling him where we had been, what about, and how well we had succeeded; he testified abundance of satisfaction that peace was not like to be interrupted, he added, when he came home his people told him, we had passed through their town, but that we had not informed them of our business.

This

This furnishes us with an instance of the *Punctilio* the *Indians* constantly treat travellers with, the people though earnestly desiring to know our commission, would not take the liberty to ask us. This night our fellow traveller lodged with his occasional wife in a corner of our cabin, and in the morning would have taken her with him at our expence, to the great vexation of Mr *Weisar*, who thought it intolerable that an intruder should gratifie his private inclinations to the shortning of our necessary provisions, already insufficient; as we did not take much pains to conceal this resentment, he had determined to part with her, though with much regret, and accordingly left her when we crossed the branch, giving her a farewell shout; we heard this with much joy, and I believe it was as well for the parties.

8th, We continued our journey without meeting any thing worth remarking, the ground we had passed rode over in our way out, and had lodged at the very creek we spent this night at.

9th. We travelled to a fine creek big enough to drive two mills, we stoped for this night at the foot of a great hill, cloathed with large *Magnolia*, 2 feet diameter and 100 feet high; perfectly straight, shagbark-hickery, chesnut and chesnut oak. This is like a bridge between the N. E. and N. W. branches of *Susquehanah*: here is also a spring from whence the wa..r runs to both branches.

K 2

10th *August*, We set out, the sun half an our high, travelled along a rich hill side, where we obferv'd a pretty many rocks, then down to a *Licking-place* by 8, where our intruder who was a good way before us fhot at an Elk, and having wounded him, purfued him feveral hours. We waited his return till 2 o'clock, *Lewis Evans* took an obfervation here, and found the lat. 41. a half. Set out again at 3, and travelled over fine rich ground by a creek where we lodged. I took a fancy to afcend 2 thirds of the height of a neighbouring hill, in the way I came to abundance of loofe ftones, and very craggy rocks, which feemed to threaten impending ruin, the foil was black and very rich, full of great wild ftinging nettles, as far as I went I rolled down feveral loofe ftones to make a path for my more expeditious return. This I found the *Indians* much difturbed at, for they faid it would infallibly produce rain the next day, I told them I had fufficient experience, it fignified nothing, for it was my common practice to roll down ftones from the top of every fteep hill, and could not recollect that it ever rained the next day, and that I was almoft fure to morrow would be a very fair day.

11th, We got out before fun rife, and rode over very good bottoms of *Linden*, *Poplar* and *Elm*, we killed a rattle fnake, and foon after found a patch of *Chamerododendron*, at 8 we came to a creek winding from between the

mountains

mountains on the left, then along a level to
another from the right, which we croſſed to
our former cabin. Quickly after we reached
a bad hill, where I firſt found the *Ginſeng* in
th s journey, the ſoil was black and light, with
flat ſtones facing the eaſt, there we paſſed by
9, then over a bottom of laurel and pine to a
creek we had ſeveral times croſſed, when ob-
ſtructed as frequently we were by hills, keep
ing cloſe to the water on the ſide we were riding. At 10 we left this creek for the ſake
ɔ a ſhorter way than we came, for this pur-
poſe we kept a S. courſe to the top of a high
but very poor hill, which we reached about a qr.
after eleven, and had a proſpect ſtill to a gap
we were to paſs to the river; the northſide of
this hill was cloathed with tall ſpruce, while
pine and beech, the top with cheſnut, ſcrubby
oak, and huckle berries, the S. ſide with ſhrub,
honeyſuckles &c. Our way was now over a
poor pebble ſtoney vale of laurel, ſpruce firr,
pine, cheſnut, and huckle berries, to a *Run* of
water; where we dined on parched meal
mixed with water. We left that place at half
an hour after one, and ſoon found ourſelves
much diſtreſſed by the broad flat ſtones on the
ſide of the hill, our way lay over. Our horſes.
could hardly ſtand, but even ſlipt on their ſides
on our left a rivulet ruſhed from a precipice,
and the mountains were ſo ſteep and cloſe to
its ſides, that we were oblidged to climb to the
top

top of that on the weft; here we fuffered our horfes to reft while we gathered huckle berries to eat, we travelled on the top a good way all ftony to the point, which was very narrow, and the flat ftones on each fide turned up like the ridge of a houfe, this reminded me of *Dr. Burnets Theory*, and his ingenious *Hypothefis*, to account for the formation of mountains. The defcent was moderate, the land middling, oak, chefnut and huckle-berries: we found a *Run* here and repofed ourfelves for this night, having fupped on venifon, fhot by our *Indians* who left us on the hill that evening. It was fair and plea-fant, and the great green grafs-hopper began to fing (*Catedidift*) thefe were the firft I ob-ferved this year. Before day break it began to rain, it lafted about an hour and then ceaf-ed. The *Indians* infifted that was caufed by the ftones I rolled down 2 days ago, I told the *Antecoque Indians* if their obfervations had any truth it fhould have been the day before, which was remarkably fair. To this he cuningly replyed, that our *Almanacks* often prognofti-cated on a day, and yet the rain did not come within two days.

12*th*, This day, the land produced middling oak, pitch, pine, and huckleberries, fometimes pebbles and a fhallow foil. We dined on venifon (partly our own, and partly given us by the *Indians*) at a deferted town about 7 miles off; this is called the *French* town, from a *French* woman

woman who married a *Delawar Indian*, and
conformed to their manners; she left several
children behind her, who were now come to
look after their horses and break the young
ones. It rained very fast for an hour, and in
the midst of it about half a score of the
5 *Nations*, who had been on the back of *S.
Carolina* to fight the *Catawba's*, passed very
fast through the town with one poor female
prisoner, they shouted couragiously, but we
learnt no particulars of this great enterprize:
about 3 it cleared up, we crossed the creek and
travelled about 10 miles, most of the way
good rich land, extensive bottoms and high
grass: I saw one lovely white *Lychnus* 5 feet
high. Near night it began to rain, and we
made a bark cabin, which kept us pretty dry,
the rain continued all night with thunder.

13th, It cleared up early in the morning. We
moved forward to our first cabin, where we
dined on parched meal, which is some of the
best *Indians* travelling provision. We had of
it 2 bags, each a gallon, from the *Indians* at
Onondago, the preparation of it is thus. They
take the corn and parch it in hot ashes, till
it becomes brown, then clean it, pound it in a
mortar and sift it; this powder is mixt with
sugar. About 1 qr. of a pint, diluted in a pint
of water, is a hearty traveling dinner, when
100 miles from any inhabitants: about 2 hours
after seting out we came near the river. Here

5 of us rode over a great rattle fnake unfeen and unhurt. I perceived him juft as my mare was over him; a little further we faw another juft by us. We travelled till near fun fet, when 2 of our *Indians* were taken with a bad fit of an ague, this obliged us to encamp by the river, where our horfes had excellent food. At about 20 rods from it I faw a bank much higher up, being near 30 feet perpendicular above the furface of the water, raifed gradually to this height by the frequent floods, which this weftern branch is much fubject too. Thus by fand continually heaped upon the firm fand, it is become a ftrong fand bank.

14*th*, We paffed through an old town, where we found plumbs, peaches, and noble clufters of large grapes growing, very deep in fand, left about them by the flood I mentioned juft now; a little farther the land was rich and low, covered with high weeds and grafs, with locuft, linden, walnut and elm, the higher land with elm and oak. At 11 o'clock we reached *Shamokin*, here we boiled dumplins and had plenty of water melons; we ftayed all night.

15*th*, Next day by noon we came to *Moho-nyoy*, where we ftayed dinner, in the afternoon we rode over fome ftony poor land, then piney, white oak, and fome middling land.

16*th*, This morning I was entertained with the Mufical howling of a wolf, which I had

not

not heard for many years, but my companions were too faft afleep to hear it, we fet out early and by one had croffed the 3 ridges of the *blue mountains,* and the 2 fpruce vales, were the branches of *Swatara* ran, and dined in St. *Anthonys Wildernefs,* as *Count Zinzendorf* has named it. We mounted again at 2 and climbed up the S. ridge, and at the top let our horfes reft, for they were cover'd with fweat. In the mean time we look'd for water, but found none, in this fearch we found an *Indian Squaw* drying huckle berries. This is done by fetting 4 forked fticks, in the ground, about 3 or 4 feet high, then others a-crofs, over them the ftalks of our common *Jacea* or *Saratula,* on thefe lie the berries, as malt is fpread on the hair cloth over the kiln. Underneath fhe had kindled a fmoke fire, which one of her children was tending. The quantity of their huckle berries growing on and between thefe ridges, is prodigious, the top of the S. ridge is pretty good land, and affords a fine profpect of the great and fertile vale of *Tulpihocken,* the ridge itfelf is pleafant. When we had refted ourfelves and our poor tired horfes, we lead them moft of the way for 20 miles, this gave us an opportunity of gathering what quantity we pleafed of their berries, tho' we eat rather more than I thought we might fafely venture on, yet we found no ill confequence from our excefs. When we were defcended we had but

L   2 miles

2 miles to a house, where we lodged, it rained fast in the evening and great part of the night itself. And we heartily congratulated ourselves on the enjoyment of good bread, butter and milk, in a comfortable house, and clean straw to sleep on, free from fleas.

17th, Though my mare was so lame, she had not stirred 20 yards all night, yet we got this day by noon to Mr *Conrad Weisars*; but under the difficulty of carrying my baggage good part of the way on my back, besides being scarcely able to get her along: when she came into the pasture, she stretched herself at full length and rose no more for 24 hours. In the afternoon I spent my time on Mr *Weisar's* high hill, gathering of seeds: here the great vale and blue mountains form a lovely prospect.

18th, I borrowed a horse of Mr *Weisar*, and set up all night at *Monatawony*.

19th, Before sunset, I had the pleasure of seeing my own house and family: I found them in good health, and with a sincere mind, I returned thanks to the almighty power, that had preserved us all.

In this journey into the heart of a country, still in the possession of it's original inhabitants: I could not help sometimes to divert the length of the way by reflecting on their manners, their complection so different from ours, and their Traditions: this led me to conjecture at their origin, or whence

whence they came into *America*, and at what time. Perhaps it may be equally hard to disprove or to prove that they were originally placed here by the same creator who made the world, as soon as this part of it became habitable, for it is reasonable to suppose the almighty power provided for the peopling of this, as well as of the other side of the globe, by a suitable stock of the human species.

However if we are to account for their passing from what is called the old world, there are many relations of voyages hither from the North of *Europe*, previous to that of *Columbus*, which though dark and uncertain, are neither evidently fabulous, nor even improbable from either the length or difficulties of the way. That the *Norwegians*, the possessors of *Iceland*, for many ages past had colonies in *Greenland*, is a fact too well attested to admit a doubt, from *Greenland* the short passage cross *Daon's Streights* brings us into the continent of *America*. If these colonies be put out of the question, it is scarce possible to think, that of the numerous fleets with which the *Danes* and *Norwegians* terrified continually the rest of *Europe*, none tempted by the hopes of gain, or drove by stress of weather, should ever fall in with the coasts of *Newfoundland* or *Gulph of St. Lawrence*. If it be objected that the navigators of those

times

times were too unskilfull to attempt such a
discovery, does it not furnish us with a reason
to account for its being made by chance. If
this passage was ever publickly known, which is
more probable it was not, might not the knowledge of it be lost as that to *Greenland*, and
can we be sure that the *Greenland* of the *Norwegians* was not more to the southward of
that country now so called. I am not ignorant that these traditions of the *Norwegian*
colonies, as well as many others to the same
point, particularly that of prince *Madoc* has
been treated as meer fiction ; but let us not
forget that *Herodotus's* account of the doub-
ling the Cape of *Good Hope* has been treated so
likewise too, tho' the fact be now established to
the degree of moral certainty.

Again, it is not unlikely but there may be
land most of the way from *America* to *Japan*,
at least islands, separated only by narrow chan-
nels, and in sight, or nearly so, of one another.
I have been lately informed of an *Indian* woman, well known by a person in *Canada*, and
after an interval of many years met again by
the same person in *Chinese Tartary* ; he could
not be convinced she was the same, till by
discourse he had with her, she told him, that
being made captive by a neighbouring nation,
she had during many years been trans-
ferred by captivity, sale, or gift, from one
nation to another till she was brought where
he

he found her. If this be true it muſt be *Continent* moſt of the way.

Another manner of peopling this ſide of the earth, particularly *S. America*, might be by ſome veſſels of the *Egyptians*, *Phænicians*, or *Carthaginians* being blown off the coaſt of *Guinea* to that of *Brazil*, or the *Antilles* in their courſe, to or from the cape of *Good-Hope*; in which caſe, for want of thoſe *Arts* and *Sciences* which are not to be found in *America*, before it's plantation by the whites, and which are ſeldom to be met with in a ſhips crew, they muſt take to that way of life our *Indians* now follow. This conjecture is the more probable, as even in the ſtate of perfection, the art of navigation is now arrived at, this accident is often unavoidable.

But whatever was their origin, our ſix nations may be now thus characteriſed: they are a ſubtile, prudent, and judicious people in their councils, indefatigable, crafty, and revengeful in their wars, the men lazy and indolent at home, the women continual ſlaves, modeſt, very loving, and obedient to their husbands. As to the natural diſpoſition of theſe *Nations*, they are grave, ſolid, and ſtill in their recreations, as well as in their councils. The *Delawar's* and *Suſquehanah's*, on the contrary, are very noiſy in their recreations, and loud in diſcourſe; but all when in liquor, whether men or women, take the liberty of
ſhouting

shouting, singing, and dancing at an extravagant rate, till the operations of the liquor cease; or being wearied they fall asleep.

The six nations enjoy the character of being the most warlike people in *N. America*, this they have acquired by the uninterrupted state of war, they have continued in probably near 200 years, and which has been attended with such success, that has made them the dread of people above 1000 miles distant. It cannot however be supposed, but they have frequently met with several checks, especially since the *French* assisted all their enemies openly near these 100 years past.

Their wars were formerly carried on with much more cruelty then of late, their prisoners who had the misfortune to fall into their hands, being generally tortured to death, now their numbers being very much diminished by constant wars, with both distant and neighbouring nations, and perhaps a good deal partly by the spirituous liquors, and diseases the Europeans have brought among them. They very politically strive to strengthen themselves not only by alliances with their neighbours, but the prisoners they take; they are almost always accepted by the relations of a warrior slain in his place, and thus a boy of 15, is sometimes called father by men of 30. This naturalizes them of course, and unites them into the tribe the deceased belonged to. This

custom

cuſtom is as antient as our knowledge of them, but when their number of warriours was more than twice as many as now, the relations would more frequently refuſe to adopt the priſoner, but rather chuſe to gratify their thirſt of revenge.

Their religious notions are very confuſed and much mixed with ſuperſtition. Yet they ſeem not only to acknowledge a deity, but e-ven to worſhip him in unity and ſpirit. What benefits they receive, they aſcribe to a di-vine power. They have ſtrange notions of ſpirits, conjuration, and witchcraft : theſe are agreeable to their blindneſs, and want of proper education among them, for I have al-ways obſerved, that the belief of ſupernatu-ral powers in a meer man, generally prevails in proportion to a Perſon's ignorance.

A Letter from Mr. KALM, *a Gentleman of* Sweden, *now on his Travels in* America, *to his Friend in* Philadelphia ; *containing a particular Account of the* GREAT FALL *of* Niagara.

S I R, *Albany, Sep.* 2, 1750.

AFter a pretty long journey made in a ſhort time, I am come back to this town. You may remember, that when I took my leave of you, I told you, I would this ſummer, if time permitted, take a view of *Niagara* FALL,
esteemed

efteemed one of the greateft curiofities in the World. When I came laft year from *Quebec*, you enquir'd of me feveral particulars concerning this fall; and I told you what I heard of it in *Canada*, from feveral *French* gentlemen who had been there: but this was ftill all hearfay; I could not affure you of the truth of it, becaufe I had not then feen it myfelf, and fo it could not fatisfy my own, much lefs your curiofity. Now, fince I have been on the fpot, it is in my power to give you a more perfect and fatisfactory defcription of it.

After a fatiguing travel, firft on horfeback thro' the country of the *Six Indian Nations*, to *Ofwego*, and from thence in a Canoe upon lake *Ontario*, I came on the 12th of *Auguft* in the evening to *Niagara* fort. The *French* there feemed much perplexed at my firft coming, imagining I was an *Englifh* officer, who under pretext of feeing *Niagara* Falls, came with fome other view; but as foon as I fhew'd them my paffports, they chang'd their behaviour, and received me with the greateft civility. *Niagara* Fall is fix *French* leagues from *Niagara* Fort. you firft go three leagues by water up *Niagara* river, and then three leagues over the carrying place. As it was late when I arriv'd at the Fort, I could not the fame day go to the Fall, but I prepar'd myfelf to do it the next morning. The commandant

of

of the Fort, Monſr. *Beaujon*, invited all the officers and gentlemen there to ſupper with him. I had read formerly almoſt all the authors that have wrote any thing about this Fall; and the laſt year in *Canada*, had made ſo many enquiries about it, that I thought I had a pretty good Idea of it, and now at ſupper, requeſted the gentlemen to tell me all they knew and thought worth notice relating to it, which they accordingly did. I obſerved that in many things they all agreed, in ſome things they were of different opinions, of all which I took particular notice. When they had told me all they knew, I made ſeveral queries to them concerning what I had read and heard of it, whether ſuch and ſuch a thing was true or not? and had their anſwers on every circumſtance. But as I have found by experience in my other travels, that very few obſerve nature's works with accuracy, or report the truth preciſely, I cannot now be entirely ſatisfied without ſeeing with my own eyes whenever 'tis in my power, Accordingly the next morning, being the 13th of *Auguſt*, at break of day, I ſet out for the Fall. The commandant had given orders to two of the Officers of the Fort to go with me and ſhew me every thing, and alſo ſent by them an order to Monſr. *Jonqueire*, who had liv'd ten years by the carrying-place, and

M   knew

knew every thing worth notice of the Fall,
better than any other perfon, to go with
me, and fhew and tell me whatever he knew.
A little before we came to the carrying-place,
the water of *Niagara* River grew fo rapid,
that four men in a light birch canoe, had
much difficulty to get up thither. Canoes can
go half a league above the beginning of the
carrying-place, tho' they muft work againft
a water extremely rapid ; but higher up it is
quite impoffible, the whole courfe of the
water for two leagues and a half up to the great
Fall, being a feries of fmaller Falls, one under
another, in which the greateft canoe or Battoe
would in a moment be turn'd upfide down.
We went afhore therefore, and walk'd over
the carrying-place, having befides the high
and fteep fide of the river, two great hills to
afcend one above the other. Here on the
carrying-place I faw above 200 *Indians*, moft
of them belonging to the *Six Nations*, bufy in
carrying packs of furs, chiefly of deer and
bear, over the carrying-place. You would
be furpriz'd to fee what abundance of thefe
things are brought every day over this place.
An *Indian* gets 20 pence for ever pack he
carries over, the diftance being three leagues.
Half an hour paft 10 in the morning we came
to the great Fall, which I found as follows.
to the river (or rather ftrait,)runs here from
S. S. E. to N. N. W and the rocks of the great
Fall

Fall croffes it, not in a right line; but form-
ing almoft the figure of a femicircle or horfe
fhoe. Above the Fall, in the middle of the
river is an ifland, lying alfo S. S. E. and
N. N. W. or parallel with the fides of the
river; its length is about 7 or 8 french arpents
(an arpent being 180 feet.) the lower end of
this Ifland is juft at the perpendicular edge of
the Fall.   On both fides of this ifland runs all
the water that comes from the lakes of *Canada*,
viz. Lake *Superior*, lake *Mifchigan*, lake
Huron, and lake *Erie*, which you know are
rather fmall feas than lakes, and have befides
a great many large rivers that empty their
water in them, of which the greateft part comes
down this *Niagara* Fall. Before the water
comes to this ifland, it runs but flowly, com-
par'd with its motion when it approaches
the ifland, where it grows the moft rapid
water in the World, runing with a furprizing
fwiftnefs before it comes to the Fall; it is
quite white, and in many places is thrown
high up into the air! The greateft and ftrongeft
battoes would here in a moment be turn'd
over and over.   The water that goes down on
the weft fide of the ifland, is more rapid, in
greater abundance, whiter, and feems almoft
to outdo an arrow in fwiftnefs. When you are
at the Fall, and look up the river, you may
fee, that the river above the Fall is every
where exceeding fteep, almoft as the fide of a

hill

hill. When all this water comes to the very
Fall, there it throws itself down perpendicular! It is beyond all belief the surprize
when you see this! I cannot with words
express how amazing it is! You cannot see
it without being quite terrified; to behold
so vast a quantity of water falling headlong
from a surprising height! I doubt not
but you have a desire to learn the exact
height of this great Fall. Father *Hennepin*,
supposes it 600 Feet perpendicular; but
he has gained little credit in *Canada*; the
name of honour they give him there, is *un
grand Menteur*, or *The great Liar*; he writes
of what he saw in places where he never was.
'tis true he saw this Fall: but as it is the way
of some travellers to magnify every thing, so
has he done with regard to the fall of *Niagara*. This humour of travellers, has occasioned me many disappointments in my travels, having seldom been so happy as to find
the wonderful things that had been related by
others. For my part, who am not fond of
the *Marvellous*, I like to see things just as
they are, and so to relate them. Since Father
Hennepin's time, this Fall by all the accounts
that have been given of it, has grown less and
less; and those who have measur'd it with
mathematical instruments find the perpendicular fall of the water to be exactly 137 feet.
Monsr. *Morandrier*, the king's engineer in
Canada,

Canada, assured me, and gave it me also under his hand, that 137 Feet was precisely the height of it; and all the *French* Gentlemen that were present with me at the Fall, did agree with him, without the least contradiction: it is true, those who have try'd to measure it with a line, find it sometimes 140, sometimes 150 feet, and sometimes more; but the reason is, it cannot that way be measured with any certainty, the water carrying away the Line.——When the water is come down to the bottom of the rock of the Fall, it jumps back to a very great heighth in the air; in other places it is white as milk or snow; and all in motion like a boiling chaldron.——You may remember, to what a great distance *Henepin* says the noise of this great Fall may be heard. All the gentlemen who were with me, agreed, that the fartheft one can hear it, is 15 leagues, and that very seldom. When the air is quite calm, you can hear it to *Niagara* Fort; but seldom at other times, because when the wind blows, the waves of Lake *Ontario* make too much noise there against the Shore.——They inform'd me, that when they hear at the Fort the noise of the Fall, louder than ordinary, they are sure a North East Wind will follow, which never fails: this seems wonderful, as the Fall is South West from the Fort: and one would imagine it to be rather a sign of a contrary wind. Some-

times,

times, 'tis faid, the Fall makes a much greater noife than at other times; and this is look'd upon as a certain mark of approaching bad weather, or rain; the *Indians* here hold it always for a fure fign. When I was there, it did not make an extraordinary great noife: juft by the Fall, we could eafily hear what each other faid, without fpeaking much louder than common when converfing in other places. I do not know how others have found fo great a noife here, perhaps it was at certain times, as abovementioned. From the Place where the water falls, there rife abundance of vapours, like the greateft and thickeft fmoak, fometimes more, fometimes lefs: thefe vapours rife high in the air when it is calm, but are difpers'd by the wind when it blows hard. If you go nigh to this vapour or fog, or if the wind blows it on you, it is fo penetrating, that in a few minutes you will be as wet as if you had been under water. I got two young *Frenchmen* to go down, to bring me from the fide of the Fall at the bottom, fome of each of the feveral kinds of herbs, ftones and fhells they fhould find there; they returned in a few minutes, and I really thought they had fallen into the water: they were obliged to ftrip themfelves quite naked, and hang their clothes in the fun to dry. When you are on the other Eaft fide of the Lake *Ontario*, a great many leagues from the Fall,

you

you may, every clear and calm morning see the vapours of the Fall rising in the air ; you would think all the woods thereabouts were set on fire by the *Indians*, so great is the apparent smoak. In the same manner you may see it on the West side of the lake *Erie*, a great many leagues off.

Several of the *French* gentlemen told me, that when birds come flying into this fog or smoak of the fall, they fall down and perish in the Water ; either because their wings are become wet, or that the noise of the fall astonishes them, and they know not were to go in the Dark : but others were of opinion, that seldom or never any bird perishes there in that manner ; because, as they all agreed, among the abundance of birds found dead below the fall, there are no other sorts then such as live and swim frequently in the water ; as swans, geese, ducks, water-hens, teal, and the like. And very often great flocks of them are seen going to destruction in this manner : they swim in the river above the fall, and so are carried down lower and lower by the water, and as water-fowl commonly take great delight in being carry'd with the stream, so here they indulge themselves in enjoying this pleasure so long, till the swiftness of the water becomes so great, that 'tis no longer possible for them to rise, but they are driven down the precipice, and perish. They are observ'd when they
draw

draw nigh the fall, to endeavour with all their might, to take wing and leave the water, but they cannot. In the months of *September* and *October*, such abundant quantities of dead waterfowl are found every morning below the Fall, on the shore, that the garrison of the fort for a long time live chiefly upon them; besides the fowl, they find also several sorts of dead fish, also deer, bears, aud other animals which have tried to cross the water above the fall; the larger animals are generally found broken to pieces. Just below the fall the water is not rapid, but goes all in circles and whirls like a boiling pot; which however doth not hinder the *Indians* going upon it in small canoes a fishing; but a little lower begins the smaller fall. When you are above the fall, and look down, your head begins to turn: the *French* who have been here 100 times, will seldom venture to look down, without at the same time keeping fast hold of some tree with one hand.

It was formerly thought impossible for any body living to come at the Island that is in the middle of the fall: but an accident that happen'd 12 years ago, or thereabouts, made it appear otherwise. The history is this. Two *Indians* of the *Six Nations* went out from *Niagara* fort, to hunt upon an island that is in the middle of the river, or strait, above the great fall, on which there used to be abundance of deer. They took some *French* brandy with
them

them, from the fort, which they tafted feveral
times as they were going over the carrying
place ; and when they were in the canoe,
they took now and then a dram, and fo went
along up the ftrait towards the Ifland where
they propos'd to hunt; but growing fleepy,
they laid themfelves down in the canoe, which
getting loofe drove back with the ftream, farther and farther down till it came nigh that
ifland that is in the middle of the fall. Here
one of them, awakened by the noife of the fall.
cries out to the other, that they were gone!
yet they try'd if poffible to favelife. This ifland
was nigheft, and with much working they got
on fhore there. At firft they were glad; but
when they had confider'd every thing, they
thought themfelves hardly in a better ftate
than if they had gone down the fall, fince they
had now no other choice, than ei her to throw
themfelves down the fame, or to perifh with
hunger. But hard neceffity put them on in-
vention. At the lower end of the ifland the
rock is perpendicular, and no water is running
there. This ifland has plenty of wood, they
went to work directly and made a ladder or
fhrouds of the bark of lindentree, (which is
very tough and ftrong,) fo long 'till they
could with it reach the water below ; one end
of this bark ladder they tied faft to a great
tree that grew at the fide of the rock a-
bove the fall, and let the other end down

N   to

to the water. So they went down along their new-invented stairs, and when they came to the bottom in the middle of the fall, they rested a little; and as the water next below the fall is not rapid, as beforementioned, they threw themselves out into it, thinking to swim on shore. I have said before, that one part of the fall is on one side of the island, the other on the other side. Hence it is, that the waters of the two cataracts running against each other, turn back against the rock that is just under the island. Therefore, hardly had the *Indians* began to swim, before the waves of the eddy threw them with violence against the rock from whence they came. They tried it several times, but at last grew weary; and being often thrown against the rock they were much bruis'd, and the skin of their bodies torn in many places. So they were oblig'd to climb up their stairs again to the island, not knowing what to do. After some time they perceived *Indians* on the shore, to whom they cried out. These saw and pity'd them, but gave them little hopes of help: yet they made haste down to the fort, and told the commander where two of their brethren were. He persuaded them to try all possible means of relieving the two poor *Indians*; and it was done in this manner. The water that runs on the east side of this island is shallow, especially

a

a little above the island towards the eastern shore. The commandant caused poles to be made and pointed with iron: two *Indians* determined to walk to this island by the help of these poles, to save the other poor creatures, or perish themselves. They took leave of all their friends as if they were going to death. Each had two such poles in his hands, to set against the bottom of the stream, to keep them steady. So they went and got to the island, and having given poles to the two poor *Indians* there, they all returned safely to the main. Those two *Indians* who in the above mentioned manner were first brought to this island, are yet alive. They were nine days on the island, and almost starved to death.*—Now since the way to this island has been found, the *Indians* go there often to kill deer, which having tried to cross the river above the fall, were driven upon the island by the stream: but if the King of *France* would give me all *Canada*, I would not venture to go to this island; and were you to see it, Sir, I am sure you would have the same sentiment. On the west side of this island are some small islands or rocks of no consequence. The east

---

* These *Indians* had better fortune than 10 or 12 *Utowawa's* who attempting to escape here the pursuit of their Enemies of the *Six Nations*, were carried down the Cataract, by the violence of the stream and every one perished.——No part even of their Canoe being ever seen again.

side

side of the river is nearly perpendicular, the west side more sloping. In former times a part of the rock at the Fall which is on the west side of the island, hung over in such a manner, that the water which fell perpendicularly from it, left a vacancy below, so that people could go under between the rock and the water; but the prominent part some years since broke off and fell down; so that there is now no possibility of going between the falling water and the rock, as the water now runs close to it all the way down.——The breadth of the Fall, as it runs into a semicircle, is reckon'd to be about 6 Arpents. The island is in the middle of the Fall, and from it to each side is almost the same breadth: the breadth of the island at its lower end is two thirds of an Arpent, or thereabouts.——Below the Fall in the holes of the rocks, are great plenty of Eels, which the *Indians* and *French* catch with their hands without other means; I sent down two *Indian* boys, who directly came up with about twenty fine ones.—— Every day, when the Sun shines, you see here from 10 o'clock in the morning to 2 in the afternoon, below the Fall, and under you, when you stand at the side over the Fall, a glorious rainbow and sometimes two rainbows, one within the other.

I was

I was so happy to be at the Fall on a fine clear day, and it was with great delight I view'd this rainbow, which had almost all the colours you see in a rainbow in the air. The more vapours, the brighter and clearer is the rainbow. I saw it on the East side of the Fall in the bottom under the place where I stood, but above the water. When the wind carries the vapours from that place, the rainbow is gone, but appears again as soon as new vapours come. From the Fall to the landing above the Fall, where the canoes from Lake *Erie* put on shore, (or from the Fall to the upper end of the carrying-place) is half a mile. Lower the canoes dare not come, lest they should be obliged to try the fate of the two *Indians*, and perhaps with less success.———
They have often found below the Fall pieces of human bodies, perhaps of drunken *Indians*, that have unhappily came down the Fall. I was told at *Oswego*, that in *October*, or thereabouts, such plenty of feathers are to be found here below the Fall, that a man in a days time can gather enough of them for several beds, which feathers they said came off the birds kill'd at the Fall. I ask'd the *French*, if this was true? They told me they had never seen any such thing; but that if the feathers were pick'd off the dead birds, there might be such a quantity. The *French* told me, they had often thrown whole great trees into

the

the water above, to see them tumble down
the Fall. They went down with surprising
swiftness, but could never be seen afterwards;
whence it was thought there was a bottomless
deep or abyss just under the Fall. I am also
of Opinion, that there must be a vast deep
here; yet I think if they had watched very
well, they might have found the trees at some
distance below the Fall. The rock of the
Fall consists of a grey limestone.

Here you have, Sir, a short but exact description of this famous *Niagara* cataract : you may
depend on the truth of what I write. You
must excuse me if you find in my acccount,
no extravagant wonders. I cannot make nature otherwise than I find it. I had rather it
should be said of me in time to come, that
I related things as they were, and that all is
found to agree with my Description; than to
be esteem d a false Relater. I have seen
some other things in this my journey, an account of which I know would gratify your
curiosity ; but time at present will not permit
me to write more.; and I hope shortly to
see you.   I am, *&c.*

PETER KALM.

F I N I S.